This is Personal.

From the Heart of an Intercessor

Tieka M. Bonaparte

Copyright © 2019, Tieka Bonaparte – All Rights Reserved

This is Personal: In the Heart of an Intercessor

I Come Alive Movement / Created 4 Purpose

For more information about Tieka Bonaparte visit:
www.faithwordoutreach.org

ISBN: 9781702446617

Cover Design: I Come Alive Series
Editing: The Birthing Movement, Inc.
Publisher: Tieka Bonaparte

Unless otherwise stated scripture quotations are taken from The Swindoll
Bible, New Living Translation, Copyright 1996, 2004, 2015

All rights reserved. No part of this publication may be reproduced, stored in a
retrieval system, or transmitted in any form or by any means, electronic,
mechanical, photocopying, recording, or otherwise, without the prior written
permission of the publisher/author.

Printed in the United States of America

Dedication

To my best friend, my supporter, my husband and my Pastor, Travis Bonaparte, the one whom I take this walk with on this side of heaven. You have always stood by my side, prayed with me and for me. You have never ceased to encourage me to be who God called me to be.

To my wonderful children, whom I love with all my heart and cherish dearly. I strive to leave an impartation of a lifestyle of prayer and obedience through God's word.

Ryheem (Limarh), De'Shane, Katilyn, Mason

To my loving Mom, Diane Wolfe, you have taught me to always care for others and never worry about what they do or say; forgiveness is key to another's breakthrough and I should always look at people through the lens of Christ.

Preface

Prayer is a gift from God. It is not something that we do for God, but a beautiful gift that He bestows on us as we humbly seek His presence. Our prayers when rendered develops relationship. One that flows first and foremost from an inner relationship with the Holy Spirit. *This is Personal* was born from a place of intimacy and out of a deep adoration toward our heavenly Father. A posture of yielding and making oneself vulnerable to be able to experience a greater awareness of His presence through prayer. Every book has a story and from my heart this one is told. Through His Spirit that dwells in my heart, Jesus words have become my very own, "Thy kingdom come, thy will be done!" No matter how strong or weak we feel all Christians have the kingdom of God dwelling richly within them (Luke 17:21). All Christians can receive the treasures of the kingdom of God and can come to know God intimately through a life of prayer. At its very core, prayer is the communion within the heart that occurs between God and His children. When we make God's words our own it becomes a personal treasure that we must allow the enemy or anything else to steal or rob us of such a wonderful and loving gift that Father has bestowed upon us. Prayer is personal; it is raising one's mind and heart before God. Prayer allows one to be in consistent communication with God, to adore Him, to praise Him, to thank Him, to repent for our offenses, and to ask Him for our needs and the needs of others. Our hearts, our families, our communities belong to us. It is time to stop allowing the prince of this world to take and use what belongs to us against us. Prayer has been freely given to us to use as a defensive and offensive weapon to defend what has been given to us by God. The capabilities of intercessory prayer and the source behind it gives us a personal use of its commanding and declaring ways through Jesus Christ.

This is Personal speaks and dips of Matthew 6:21, *"For where your treasure is, there your heart will be also."*

Our treasure lies within Jesus Christ, and what's eternally personal to God's heart should be eternally personal to ours.

Acknowledgments

First, I would like to acknowledge God for being a great Father and for never leaving me to myself. He has kept me and carried me through this journey. Thank you, Lord, for what you are doing in this season of my life. I thank you for the hearts of the intercessors who will decide to rise up from the world and take their seat on the wall before your Throne of Grace.

There will always be someone that will leave a torch for someone else to pick up. In this case, my grandparents the greatest examples in my life, left behind the greatest torch of them all love, which shall burn forever through my prayers. The two of you cared for me and loved me deeply. You showed me the way to embrace and love others through the lens of Jesus Christ. I am forever grateful that God thought enough of me to place me in your lineage. I will forever honor and treasure our time together.

The Late Jacob Wolfe (Sr) and Lula Wright Wolfe

Thanks to my amazing and wonderful church family, Faith Word Outreach Ministries, who always pray my strength up in the Lord.

May we continue to grow together, spread the name of Jesus, and most of all continue to stand in prayer as one, so that the Father's will shall forever be glorified.

Table of Contents

Introduction 1

Chapter 1: The Author and Finisher 13

Chapter 2: A Heart to Pray 49

Chapter 3: The Battlefield 113

Chapter 4: Breaking Barriers...................................143

Chapter 5: His Glory Be Known 153

Conclusion...161

Final Thoughts 175

About the Author 179

-Intercessor-

One who acts in faith by lining up his/her heart with God's heart for a situation or person.

Introduction
From the Heart of an Intercessor

You saw me before I was born. Every day of my life was recorded in your book. Every moment was laid out before a single day had passed. How precious are your thoughts about me, O God.

Ps 139:16-17

These are two of my favorite verses in the Bible, because it signifies that we are an open book before the Lord, He knows the end from our beginning, and there is no one that knows us better than Him. These verses also give us the assurance of His great love and care. They speak to us boldly that God has a well thought out plan for our lives and there's nothing we can do or even go through that will catch Him by surprise. God took the time to detail our purpose and our call before we were thought about by our earthly parents. As individuals we were created by His hands to be different and unique, but still fitting enough with each other to help build His Kingdom. We are opened before His eyes, penned by His love and He has never ceased working out our salvation.

God's great love brought forth our first heartbeat. He spoke life into us, and if we never identify the voice of another, we should always be able to identify His voice because it was the very first voice that we ever heard.

I believe every word of purpose that He spoke inside of us brings forth the breath of life; a called assignment, and by obtaining this book you most likely know that you have a calling or an unction in your heart for the assignment of the ministry of intercession. I personally believe that all effective intercession begins in the heart of God. A ministry birthed through God's will to bring hearts back to Him through prayer. When God wants to bring forth revival to the earth, He often works through His servants to perform what He wants to manifest.

Ever since I was a young girl, I have always prayed to God to be someone that could bring people together and create change in this world. As I was asleep one night, God took me on a journey. I heard Jesus say follow me and as I began to follow Him, I saw people seated as if they were waiting to be served. As we got in front of each person Jesus stood waiting as I knelt to place a new pair of shoes on their feet and spoke a word of prayer over their lives. In this dream we didn't stop replacing shoes and praying until everyone got what they needed. From that visitation from the Lord, I awoke with a passion to serve, pray and spread the gospel to all ears that would incline themselves to hear and listen.

Prayer has become my campout fighting ground for the many souls I am connected with or have come in contact with on the daily. In this place, this campground; I pray others would receive a love that would heal their hearts which would enable and allow them to remove any hindrances, barriers and all things that would continue to keep them from the promises of God. I pray that God would help them to walk in peace with the newness He wants to give to them.

Through faith, communing with God and much prayer, I have seen the great love of the Father compel the hearts of many. I have seen God's healing power work through sick bodies and with great amazement I have even gotten the pleasure of watching in awe as wellness manifested from prayer that aligned itself with the will and heart of the Father. I tell you there is nothing more joyous than bringing someone's name before the altar; to the one who has the ability to instantly change our circumstances. I have stood in astonishment and watched God's hands revive, strengthen, and touch the hearts of those who have grown weary or lost touch and awareness of His presence. Communing with the Father, basking in His love and praying out of faith activates the eyes of an intercessor and enables them to see the work of His hands move in all of His glory.

Prayer brings forth the awareness and knowledge that our God (who so graciously created, sacrificed his son, and saved us) will always love us and longs to see nothing but the best for His children.

Prayer was instilled in the heart of man from day one. It enables us to hear the whisper of God calling out to our hearts. Just take a moment and look at how great He is. God created a way for us to always be able to maintain an open flow of communication between Himself and mankind. God seeks intercessors. He longs to dispense and distribute larger blessings. He longs to reveal His power, His glory, and His everlasting love.

As His children, our hearts should always carry a seed of prayer in it, ready to sprout up life through the Holy Spirit's prompting. A seed of prayer that grows and increases within our heart that says, "through Christ nothing is impossible to conceive and be birthed out if we just believe." That is what allows us to take the position of Faith and Prayer as we stand in the gap for others.

The truth is that some of us are born to Preach and some of us are born to Teach.

But, there are some of us who are born and lead to bring forth the Father's heart by praying for people, our communities, this land and nation.

On our knees is where you will find us with our hearts intertwined with the Father's heart. We are faithfully praying daily that others would be able to see His works, His favor and most of all His glory. A heart that longs to beat within and through the heart of God is an intercessor who will live and incline their ears to hear every beat of the Father's heart.

We live to birth breakthrough and to share God's great love. We desire to build bridges over the gaps, stand firm on the walls, and watch until the message is clearly ready to be released. Prayer is our battlefield from which we engage in war. It is the bridge over the trenches between God and His people.

Unfortunately, in this day and time, prayer has been silenced in many homes, forced out of schools and removed from the hearts of many, but we declare that it is time to reclaim what we have rights to.

Today is a New Day.

This is a day of return and release. This is a day and hour that we shall fight on our knees for our families, our communities, and our nation. God is calling forth a new remnant of intercessors to rise and define their time by bringing the Father's heart to this land once again. We need prayers from those who will not give up or grow silent but will press and push for those who are lost, weary, tired and just cannot seem to find their way.

Within this remnant lies the birth of breakthrough, refinement and revival which will fill the atmosphere once again through God's great love. An intercessor, driven by the vehicle of faith, will not stop praying until God's will is accomplished. Intercession is indeed a weighty profound way of extending the ministry of Jesus and partnering with him in efforts to save souls. As we dare to go before a mighty

God and contend for those around us, rending selfless prayer and lifting the needs of others into the throne room of heaven before our own needs and desires are meant.

Our Love for God and for others means so much more and it will not continue to be taken lightly but personal.

"What breaks the Father's heart, has broken ours."

It is in my hope that as you read this book, you will gain the understanding for the ministry of prayer, how to mature in it, the power behind it and the necessity of it. May the eyes of our hearts be awakened to see a move of God. This is a clarion call for all intercessors to arise and stand on their posts and become the funnel that flows from God's heart to the earth once again.

May our hearts be open and ready to receive.

Father, I pray that as your children and called vessels begin to engage in this book, allow their eyes to be opened to your truths and fully surrender to your will. Help their hearts to be able to receive understanding and knowledge as they push toward a deeper hunger for you in prayer and all other areas of their lives. May they rely on your name and remain persistent through all prayer assignments that are given to them through the Holy Spirit's leading. May they walk with the grace you have given them and step in peace as they encounter any barriers or hinderances from the enemy. Give them strength in their weakness, boldness in their voice, and courage in their stand. Let them always keep their eyes on you with a pure and clean heart as they continue to pursue and walk toward the call you have purposed for their lives. Father, stand up in them. Help them be bold and clear in vision as they pursue a lifestyle of prayer. In you Lord is where they will find refuge. They will run into your arms, as they declare that you are the Sovereign Lord and they are Kingdom children with a passion and will to pray, because of who you are. Faithful, Righteous, Holy, Meek and most of all loving. In Jesus' Holy Name, Amen.

That need that you feel and the great yielding that has been infringed upon your heart to set disciplined habits in prayer begins in the Heart of God.

1 The Author and Finisher

Looking unto Jesus the author and finisher of our faith; who for the joy that was set before him endured the cross, despising the shame, and is sat down at the right hand of the throne of God.
(Hebrews 12:2)

For us to even begin to understand the call of the ministry of prayer; intercession we must first look at what is prayer, who initiates it, and who answers it? We will determine why this call requires an act of total surrender.

Prayer is a direct communication line that allows us to talk to God. Prayer is significant, vital, imperative, essential, and critical. When we render prayer something always happens. The one thing prayer never is...is a waste of time. When we pray, we offer up worship, praise and our sacrifices to God. In prayer we sacrifice our time, offer our thoughts, and release our emotions up to God so He can do with them as He pleases.

Let me go on record by saying this now before we go any further, prayer is available to everyone and can be accessed from anyplace at any time desired. All believers are commanded to pray to God for one's self and intercede on the behalf of others. *Philippians 4:6 says, "Don't worry about anything; instead, pray about everything. Tell God what you need and thank him for all he has done."* Prayer is not graced or afford to an elite few, however some are hungrier to take their place on the walls of intercession in their generation, and by doing so the Holy Spirit has allowed them to pray and travail in the spirit with a watchman's eye.

This is Personal

The Model of Intercession – Draw near to God through his Son. (Jesus Christ)

There is only one Priest among men who can go to God in His own right and intercede for us, whom Himself does not need an intercessor. That man is Jesus Christ. Which is the reason why he said, *"I am the way, the truth and the life; no one can come to the father except through me. (John 1:6)* He is the gateway to the promises of God the Father, and He stands before Him on our behalf.

Jesus Christ prayed often for His disciples. *(John 17:6-26)* He loved them, and He prayed that they might be kept from evil. He graciously modeled how they should pray and provides five areas of focus when they prayed.

"After this manner therefore pray ye: *Our Father which art in heaven, Hallowed be thy name. Thy kingdom come, Thy will be done in earth, as it is in heaven. Give us this day our daily bread. And forgive us our debts, as we forgive our debtors. And lead us not into temptation, but deliver us from evil: For thine is the kingdom, and the power, and the glory, forever. Amen (Matthew 6:9-13 kjv)*

- That God's Name be honored (Father hallowed be your name)

- On God's eternal will (Your kingdom come)

- That His provision be given (Give us each day our daily bread)

- That God's forgiveness is granted (Forgive our sins)

- That God would deliver (Us from evil)

He took the time to train His disciples and He exhibited a life that they all could follow. His work on the cross is done, but His work in us shall go forth until the day of His return. Although Jesus is seated in heaven now, He continues to pray for those who belong to Him. We are so blessed to have a High Priest, one who forever lives to make intercession for us. He is described as our, *"Advocate with the Father." (1 John 2:1-2) [An advocate is one who stand up for, speak for or campaign on behalf of]* Jesus is the perfect intercessor because He understands our weakness without Himself being weak. Jesus lived as a man, which the Bible tells us was necessary for Him to do so that He could be our merciful and faithful High Priest. Our Lord and Savior knows what it is like to be rejected, misunderstood, misused, poor, hungry, tempted and even persecuted. We must realize that there is nothing that can happen to us that He does not understand. He prays for us, intercedes on our behalf and presents our prayers to the Father. It is through Him we can come to God and find utmost grace.

Hebrews 4:16 says, *"Let us then approach God's throne of grace with confidence, so that we may receive mercy and find grace to help us in our time of need."*

- From a personal spiritual level, I decided to do this book because early in my calling to the ministry of intercession I had no clue what it entailed. I often prayed that God would send me a mentor or another likewise intercessor, to walk me through it. Today as I reflect, I would not have chosen to get here any other way. One day in prayer I heard the Holy Spirt say, *"I am your guide and God's word is your way."* It was then that I realized my spiritual growth depended on the trust that I was developing through my relationship with Him. As I continued to read the word of God, I allowed Jesus to be my model and through the leading of the

Holy Spirit, He guided and directed me to dig deeper in prayer and seek out what God willed for me to do. I had to learn and understand that prayer was more than words and beyond what anyone could teach me; it was my means of obtaining God's solutions to the situations I brought before His throne. By trusting in God and pushing through prayer I found that my love for Jesus and my dependency in Him helped me to evolve and continue to reach deeper depths in my relationship with Him as I interceded on behalf of others. Sometimes God will allow us to experience things in life that will groom us for His serves:

- Hurt and rejection

- Misuse by leadership

- The abandonment by those you thought was sent to help you.

"Man may be used as the tool to distribute the lesson, but no man can take the credit for the revelation and healing behind the experience."

As I began trusting in God and letting the vehicle of faith transport my life, I began to realize that Jesus was my example in everything. It gave me the assurance that Abba Father, my daddy would not allow me to lack, but I could come to Him and to ask for provisions and needs not only for myself but for others who were in my reach. As I continued to build myself up in Him, He allowed me to connect with other intercessors, and even a mentor that spoke into my life God's great love and how He wanted me to continue to position myself in prayer. When I removed what I wanted and trusted in His will, He sent the help because I asked for what he willed.

This is Personal

Matthew 7:7 says, "Ask, and it will be given to you; seek, and you will find; knock, and it will be opened to you." However, it is important to know that prayer is not just asking and then expecting God to wave some magic wand and boom the issue is fixed. No, Prayer is about much more than that! It is about fellowshipping with God, dwelling in His presence, listening to His voice and seeking for His will to be done.

So often I am asked, "What is prayer? How do I start? What do I say?" Often my response is, "Prayer is our response to God's voice entering our hearts. Listening to what He wants to say, seeing what He wants to do and reacting according to His will." By dwelling in His presence, I have learned over time to return the question as such, "What does prayer mean to you and when you are in prayer what do you hear the spirit of the Lord saying?" Returning a question with a question helps one evaluate their spiritual awareness and reveal their zeal for true knowledge. Our prayer life develops from our ongoing relationship with God. When we seek Him out, He responses with the understanding we need to keep the connection flowing.

The questions that ponder us about prayer can be simply answered from the appliance of it. When we stop and just talk to God it is considered prayer. Indulging yourself in a conversation with God has a way of conditioning the heart, refining the speech, and rebooting the ear canal in the spirit.

With much care and dwelling in His presence we can learn to embrace God's voice, concerning our lives and the lives of others, which will allow us to answer our own question in this manner. With a daily conditioned heart, His will becomes the basis of our prayers.

This is Personal

There is no wrong or right way to pray. Our individual relationship with Jesus is different but the same. He is the only one who can save, but the way He delivers us and where He rescued us may differ. Prayers can be short or long petitions, praises, questions, or even affirmations. It can be for self or on behalf of others. Prayer can be given with a joyous heart, broken heart, or a repentant heart, but all prayer should be given with sincere honor, in humility, and with a desire to surrender to His will. It can even be from the pouring out of our deepest emotions buried within our beings. Prayer is often set off with our knowledge that through Christ we are made worthy to come before God's Throne of Grace in faith that He hears our every word and desires to respond on our behalf according to His will.

Often, we make prayer much harder than it truly is. It sounds more like a chore than

This is Personal

a privilege; almost as if we are being forced to do it. Prayer should be thought of as a breathing process for the Christian soul. It is supposed to be easier to do than not to do. Prayer should be like oxygen, it should flow with consistency and ease.

The Crossroad of Faith and Confliction

About that time Hezekiah became deathly ill, and the prophet Isaiah son of Amoz went to visit him. He gave the king this message: "This is what the LORD says: 'Set your affairs in order, for you are going to die. You will not recover from this illness.'" 2 When Hezekiah heard this, he turned his face to the wall and prayed to the LORD, 3 "Remember, O LORD, how I have always been faithful to you and have served you single-mindedly, always doing what pleases you." Then he broke down and wept bitterly. Then this message came to Isaiah from the

This is Personal

LORD: [5] "Go back to Hezekiah and tell him, 'This is what the LORD, the God of your ancestor David, says: I have heard your prayer and seen your tears. I will add fifteen years to your life, [6] and I will rescue you and this city from the king of Assyria. Yes, I will defend this city. (Isaiah 38:1-6)

Sometimes we think our prayers are pointless because we know God's mind cannot be changed. He already knows what we are going through and what we need. So, why would God call us to pray if this is so? Why does He need us to pray if He is the originator of prayer and the solution to prayer? Simple...***Connection!***

God wants to talk to us; He wants to involve us in His plans. He wants us to remain (abide) in Him and stay connected. We do not know what the Lord has decreed, but scripture is clear that our prayers really do have an effect in God's plan to bring about His will. He really does

This is Personal

interact with us and respond to our intercessions. We must be careful when we enter a space like Hezekiah, not to allow the enemy to disconnect and confuse us into thinking that God doesn't care, and His mind is already made up about us. Since we serve an omniscient God, Satan will try to make you believe that if God is all knowing than what's the point. We must not be intimidated and afraid to come to Him in faith. We must remember that He is sovereign, absolute and unlimited. Gracefully through the great love He has for us, He is moved by our request and desires our fellowship.

Hezekiah did not give up instead he got his affairs in order, by deciding to turn his face to the wall. He cried out to God reminding him of his faithfulness and devotion. Often in prayer it is not us reminding God but God reminding us of His faithfulness and love as I believe wholeheartedly, He did on

This is Personal

the behalf of Hezekiah. This brought about self-awareness for him in a time of much needed reflection.

The priority of prayer deals more with our eternal outcome than the situational outcome of what you are even praying about. Prayer is the transportation that brings us to the place that connects us to His Spirit that produces the fruit of the Spirit for our souls and for others. It also allows us to enter a place of intimacy. A place where there is a loving conversation transpiring between a child and their loving Father.

Prayer is so important, as a believer, we do not get the option to pray or not to pray. It is our spiritual umbilical cord that flows between us and heaven. Through this cord, we can communicate with our heavenly Father. Through prayer, we talk, listen, receive instruction and direction from the source of our lives. Prayer is vital for our spiritual health and we are commanded to pray not just for ourselves but for others in the Spirit and in any occasion.

Ephesians 6:18 says, "And pray in the Spirit on all occasions with all kinds of prayers and requests. With this in mind, be alert and always keep on praying for all the Lord's people."

Beginning to End

The Bible tells us that the need that causes us to turn to God, that the inner impulse to pray, is really a response to God speaking to us. We see this in the first ever example of prayer in the Bible. *The man and his wife heard the sound of the Lord God as he was walking in the garden in the cool of the day, and hid from the Lord God among the trees of the garden. But the Lord God called to the man "Where are you?"* (Genesis 3:8-9) Our prayer life is God calling out the where are you in us. It is His Spirit calling out to you to commune and fellowship with Him.

Often, I have felt the need to pray for someone because their name came into my spirit or a vision of their face came across my mind. While we may think it is the initiative of our own, it is really God Himself seeking to awaken the spirit of intercession in you. He is up to something and He wants you involved.

Isaiah 46:9-10 God says, "I am God, and there is no one like me. My purpose will be established, and I will accomplish all My good pleasure"

God is sovereign and in control. It is not that God cannot work without our prayers, but He has established prayer as part of His plan for accomplishing His will on earth. What God wants to do in the world, He will do through His servants. Prayer releases the will of God, bringing His will

This is Personal

out of the spiritual realm to take effect in the natural realm. Prayer bridges the way for God's work to manifest and be released in the land. When God wants to change the course of events, He calls out an intercessor.

I looked for someone who might rebuild the wall of righteousness that guards the land. I searched for someone to stand in the gap in the wall so I wouldn't have to destroy the land, but I found no one. (Ezekiel 22:30)

God's plan will go forward with or without us. If we do not respond, He will move on to the next available, willing vessel and if we do not take our position on the wall, we will miss the blessing and the move of God, but His work will go forth and still be *accomplished.*

Not only is God moved by our prayers, but He bends His ears to listen, *"I love the Lord because he hears my voice and my prayer for mercy. Because he bends down to listen, I will pray as long as I have breath! (Psalm 116:1-2)"*

*Just for a minute imagine this- The creator of the universe bends down from heaven to get close to His precious beloved child in order to hear the prayers you whisper from your heart. He doesn't take the chance of missing one single word that is uttered. God is not only faithful in His watching, but He is also faithful in making sure He hears you.

Prayers of discouragement, loneliness, worry, times when you are afraid, or even brokenhearted. Rest assured that God is listening closely.

The truth and the reality is that your prayers will always reach the Father's ears. In fact, scripture reveals, in a deeper level, that He is searching and waiting for people to stand in the gap, so He may respond mercifully. *Yet the Lord longs to be gracious to you; therefore he will rise up to show you compassion. For the Lord is a God of justice. Blessed are all who wait for him! (Isaiah 30:18)*

Privilege in Prayer

God is so wonderful that He designed prayer this way; His will being brought forth on this earth with us involved. I want you to take a moment and think about how the Lord of Lords and King of Kings did not need you to bring His work forth, but He decided that through prayer His power would be released to accomplish His purpose and through His will we have the privilege of partaking and being active in His wonderful plans. Intercession is God's master plan to include the saints in ruling with Him in power. The mystery is in its

This is Personal

weakness, simplicity, humility, and accessibility to all.

"Prayer is a privilege given to all those who are born of God."

From the day of our salvation when we accepted Christ as our Lord and Savior, we became dead to self and Christ lives in us. *John 15:4 says, "Abide in me, and I will abide in you...* The assurance here is that although we died on the cross at Calvary with him over two-thousand years ago, we too live again because of the powerful resurrection of Christ that took place on that day. He did not just die and rose again, but He planned and secured a way to not leave us to ourselves when He returned to the right hand of the Father. Prayer is a blood-bought privilege for those who trust and treasure Jesus. As children of God, we must protect our privilege by being vigilant and on guard against anything that will take our communion time with the

This is Personal

Father away. Surrendered prayer possesses sweetness and power. The sweet aroma that form in our hearts and moves through the air with a delightful and joyous fragrance is the communion with God. It should never be smothered, but rather embraced, treasured and protected. David prayed in *Psalm 141:2* *"May my prayer be set before you like incense; may the lifting up of my hands be like the evening sacrifice.* David even went further in prayer by asking God in *verse 3* to *"Set a guard over his mouth and keep watch over the door of his lips."* Why because King David treasured the one, he had released his prayers too and he knew that his words would be protected by God. The power that has given us the authority to retain this privilege comes from the one we are speaking to, the one who adopted us, the Savior who bought us, the Holy Spirit who brings truth, seals and dwells in us.

This is Personal

Scripture says, *"When the Spirit of truth comes, he will guide you into all truth. He will not speak on his own but will tell you what he has heard. He will tell you about the future." (John 16:13)*

To some degree, in every believer, prayer is always going on inside of us as the Holy Spirit brings forth truth from indwelling in us. Let us reach for a deeper intense merge that will keep our praying heart in a submerged state of truth through His Spirit.

Within us and through us The Holy Spirit is always interceding to the Father causing our prayers to take flight. May He speak to us clearly as our hearts receive His guidance and utterance. Let us push forth in prayer unique power and never neglect or undermine its importance. Our spiritual health relies a great deal on our God given privilege to commune with the Father.

Also as intercessors, we have the privileged right to intercede intensely on the behalf of our family, friends, and those who do not yet follow Christ, in this time of uprising let us take honor in what a privilege it is to be one with the Father by way of prayer.

Created by God for Love

The fact that Intercession is often done on the behalf of others tells us that it must come from a place of love, wanting what God wants and knowing that whatever His decision, it is done in our best interest.

From the very beginning, the Bible tells us that we were made *in the image of God. (Gen 1:27)* [Image- likeness; resemblance] As we picture what that looks like we must take hold of what scripture says about Him. *1 John 4:16 says, "God is love, and those who abide in love abide in God, and God abides in them."* This means that if our

This is Personal

inner core is filled with His love, God shall be found there, which helps our outward man to reflect His image which frames us.

To bear the character and image of God is to be hardwired by His love. The more we are conformed to His image the more loving we will become and the more we will look and be like Him. As intercessors, we must first understand the love of God and the position, He gives us through Jesus Christ that loves us. Through Christ we have been given the opportunity to love ourselves and love on others.

Love can be explained as wanting the best for someone without wanting anything in return, and that is exactly what God extended to us knowing that there would never be anything that we could ever do to repay Him for His unfailing love that was given to us at the cross. The motivation behind everything God does in our lives and everything He allows to enter our lives is because of His love. God moves in our lives so that we might change, grow, and become both spiritually mature and whole in spirit, mind, and soul.

As believers and intercessors, we can have the faith to move mountains, but if we do not have love then we do not have anything. Love produces fruit in our lives and brings forth hope, joy, and peace as we walk this journey out on earth. Without love, both life and faith will remain sterile. The key to developing a loving relationship with the one to whom we pray and the one who created us for love is by accepting that we are children of His Lordship, which gives us the assurance that He loved us from before time began and that His love just does not start and stop with us, but it overflows on all mankind.

See what great love the Father has lavished on us, that we should be called children of

God! And that is what we are! The reason the world does not know us is that it did not know him. (1 John 3:1)

When we begin to seek the truth and gain knowledge of Him, His love begins to rain down on us like a shower from heaven. As His love showers us, it begins to mold our inner most being and shape our character, separating His children from the children of this world.

Jesus tells the Pharisees in the book of Matthew that the greatest commandments are *"You shall love the Lord, your God with all your heart, with all your soul and with all your mind" and "You shall love your neighbor as yourself." (Matthew 22:37-39)*

God longs for us to reflect His very nature because it is where we will find the greatest love that was ever produced. A love from a Father that gave His only begotten Son.

This is Personal

God made Christ, who never sinned, to be the offering for our sin, so that we could be made right with God through Christ. This is a picture of love. A love that covers the multitude of sins (1 Peter 4:8) is the love which flows through the blood of Jesus Christ. When in prayer this is always the place/picture that we should pray from. Love which flows from the pipeline of God's heart that connects our hearts to His that we may pray in love for ourselves and others.

Deepest Touch

Intercession is not for the faint of heart but rather for the tender and courageous of heart. Those who are touched by the reality of the surrounding unfaithfulness are likely to intercede. They are willing to do whatever God instructs them to do and they are open to His guidance and direction. When God touches their hearts, they pray immediately, fervently, and for

This is Personal

as long as they need too. They are the ones that are willing to stand in the gap on behalf of others. They understand that they must trust in God and rely on the power of prayer to bring forth His will.

"Saul also went to his home Gibeah, and with him went men of valor whose hearts God had touched." (1 Samuel 10:26)

One day in devotion and prayer I came across this scripture, and oh how it drew my attention and awakened my spirit in such an unexplainable way. My eyes were immediately drawn to the fact that our invisible, supernatural, spiritual God touched the heart of men without consumption. (To touch is to feel.) The touch of God brings forth connection as we talked about previously. The Valor men [Valor- bravery, courage, fearlessness] just wasn't spoken to, but they received a sensational touch in their hearts. God was just that close, and they were not even consumed by His glory. It is within my prayers that we, as intercessors, will be touched by the hands of God to allow Him to come so close to us that He will touch our hearts and we will not be overtaken, but divinely influence to walk with courage in the direction of His leading.

"Turned not away but face forward toward the direction of God and yield to His leading."

But when you pray, go away by yourself, shut the door behind you, and pray to your Father who is in private. Then your Father, who sees everything, will reward you. (Matthew 6:6) Some translations even say, "go into your closet, and shut the door" meaning "Shut out everything else when you pray do not let anything or allow anyone to interfere when you are in prayer. Do not be involved or influenced with thoughts about other things or people but talk only to God Himself. Allow your mind, body, and soul to be touched and influenced to keep your sights on Him. The valor men had the opportunity to walk by choice as we do. In their case they decided to stay focused on the mission at hand and yield to His authority; which allowed them to receive the touch of the Father's hand. Over the years, my experience has been that as I desire more of God, stay focused on Him and cut my ties with the world, the Father draws closer to me. *"Come close to God, and God will come close to you. Wash your hands, you sinners; purify your hearts, for your loyalty is divided between God and the world." (James 4:8)* It is only when we remove ourselves from worldly attachments, we can begin to move closer to God than we have ever been before. In our walk we must not allow ourselves to become attached to the streams of the world, but we must live a detached life. When we have been touched by God, we are able to pray without emotions and

This is Personal

judgement which in time will allow us to focus on what he has call or willed us to do in our prayer time.

Detachment is the ability of a person to observe, without judgment, their life circumstances, thoughts, relationships, and emotions of self and of others.

It is important what we do with our time because it is precious and limited. With the allotted time the valor men stayed focused and walked in confidence without distraction as we should do. Our prayer time is as important as any other time because it is a time of release (detachment) and replenish (His touch; restoration).

Surrender

Only when we lift our hearts to the Father in full surrender to His will and let go of everything, we have in mind can we begin to understand what God wants to do in our lives. In the book of Genesis chapter 2 the tree of knowledge of good and evil was a representation of an alternative God offered. It provided man with a choice: to love and serve God willingly or to rebel against Him and reject the one prohibition He had given them. Adam and Eve were given a choice to surrender when He said, *"you shall not* as opposed to *you cannot.*

You may ask what does that mean for me? Does that mean that what I have at my disposal does not belong to me?

When we surrender to God, we are simply acknowledging that what we own belongs to Him. He is the creator of life and the giver of all good things and we are the stewards [like Adam and Eve] given the responsibility of care over them. By simply giving what we have in our possession back to Him such as the time that we spend in prayer, our talents or even our money acknowledges that He is ultimately in

This is Personal

control of everything including our present circumstances. This serves as an aid to help us release in prayer whatever has been holding us bound from God's best life for us. There comes a time when we must consider the price that God paid to reclaim our lives, to buy back what was His in the first place, His creation. He stepped down from the throne to become like man to give us an example, show us direction, and above all express His everlasting love. He bore our sins and overcame death so that His children could once again have what He promised. We must realize that we are not our own, we were bought at a price and now with extended hands and an open heart of surrender we must transfer ownership of self to the one true owner Jesus Christ. We must run from the idea of the desires and disobedience to the flesh. The greater reward is before us, and that is continued fellowship and the opportunity to inherit the kingdom.

This is Personal

Surrender looks like this, *Our Father who art in heaven, hallowed be Your name, Your Kingdom come. Your will be done, on earth as it is in Heaven.* It is not about what elevates or aggrandizes you, it is about God's Kingdom being brought forth in our lives here on earth.

It is God who calls, hears and rescues. As we continue to stand in the gap for others, we must live a life of selfless desire and yield to God's service. Surrender is not a one-time commitment but an ongoing process so you can be used by Him. We must remove and give up anything that causes doubt. He possesses all control in His hands. Surrender causes us to come closer to God because what once hindered us no longer has a hold on us. God is the one who we kneel in pray before laying everything at His throne and it is through His name (Jesus) that our prayers will flow into His inner courts and rest at the Masters' feet.

This is Personal

A Prayer of Surrender

Father in heaven I thank you for all that you are, and all that you do for me. I praise you for my life, for your unfailing love, unmerited mercy and your saving grace. Lord, I surrender my mind, my imagination, my emotions, my weaknesses, my desire for human approval and my will at your disposal. I surrender every situation in my life, every relationship, every concern, every fear and every doubt. Take hold of all anxiety and worry that tries to rise up, consume me and rob me of the trust that I have in you. As I empty myself to make room for you, fill me with your Holy Spirit and all the gifts and fruits of your Spirit. Purify my desires. Help me to open my heart to you and trust in the love you so greatly shower and pour out to me. In Jesus' Name, Amen.

This is Personal

A Praying Heart is...

- Pure

- Unselfish

- Humble

- Yielding

- Believing, and

- Belongs to Christ

2 A Heart to Pray

"Consider as you pray for people that you may be the only person on earth praying for them. Do not give up on people, keep praying, knowing that God never gave up on you." You cannot change anyone, but you can always pray to the God who can change anything.

As a young girl growing up, I was very observant, I often looked at my family, my school, my church and even my community and saw a great need for prayer and a yearning for God to step in on behalf of my friends and loved ones who were going through hard times and lack. As I continued to grow up prayer slowly grew into my heart as more than a desire of what I wanted but a longing for others to be free of heartache, hurt, and pain.

Two of my greatest models and reasons why I pray so hard are my departed but beloved grandparents Jacob and Lula Wolfe. *Train up a child in the way he should go: and when he is old, he will not depart from it. (Proverbs 22:6)*

I often saw them in prayer for their children. (A family of 7 girls, 4 boys, and a host of grandchildren whom they raised as their own.) They prayed for leaders in the community and served faithfully in the local church. As a child, I often wondered why God would listen to them when He already knew what was going on around them. Couldn't He fix it if He wanted to? As I continued seeing them pray day after day and night after night, I was led to listen to their words. In my observation, I noticed that their words were built around God's faithfulness, His love, mercy and grace. Not what they needed or desired for what was going on, but their words seemed to always seek God's heart and not His hand. As I listened, I realized that chasing after God's heart was more important than seeing the move of His hands, because His hands moves for what His heart wills. My grandparents were not trying to change God's mind for their situation, but they were trying to align themselves for what He had planned to bring out through the circumstances. They were readying their selves for the answer.

This was a well taught lesson for me, how they positioned themselves in prayer helped me to align, the way I posture myself today. I soon began to ask God to help me pray in such a manner, that He would give me the heart to pray for His will to be done and not the way my mind wanted it to go. Whatever that meant for the issues at hand in my life and the lives of others, what He decided to do was best for all involved.

This is Personal

A powerful lifestyle in prayer is not a matter of knowing the right words to say, rather it is having a heart rightly positioned for God's disposal. Yes, I said, *lifestyle*. A heart that is willing to set aside its own aspirations and urges of its own and solely be used for His will and His glory every day in every way.

Intercessory Prayer should be released from a heart that trusts in God, one that does not lean on its own understanding but in all its ways submitting itself to Him on a regular basis. By letting the flow of prayer trickle down from His heart to ours allows us to guide our words with sincerity. When in prayer our words should form from a language of God's love and will, not a language of sound good - feel good flesh.

When we submerge ourselves in prayer our words may not even sound intellectual, words spoken unknown to man, and perhaps even groans from the Spirit because often we are so burdened, we do not know what we should pray, so the Holy Spirit prays on our behalf.

Through the posture of our heart, God's heart is expressed through our words. *Matthew 12:34 expresses, "For the mouth speaks what the heart is full of."* So how do we express God's heart through our words? Just like any other thing, what we feast on and digest is what will be consumed and released. In our everyday consumption we consciously and unconsciously feed and store up on things we surround ourselves with on the daily. However, we do get the choice to detach the things that don't agree with our spirits. For instance, if we read the Word of God on a regular basis and are pleased or even satisfied by its containments, then we will desire to feed constantly on it. It will eventually become part of the reservoir in our hearts as we consciously and unconsciously remember its teachings. The same goes for listening to music or even watching television, if we listen to its words and like its message then we will retain its teachings and that is what our spirit will be filled with. The more we do something or surround ourselves with it, the more it becomes the thing we know best and the knowledge that grows inside of it. Our mouths speak of what our heart (our inner core) is brimming of.

Today a lot of people seek fame, fortune, pleasurable foods, happiness or worldly gain and the love and the opinion of people in hopes that their emptiness would be filled through them, but so often they find out that what they have consumed has no sustainment at all but has actually caused them to be further suppressed into a deeper hunger. As an intercessor I've learned to always seek to feast upon God's

This is Personal

words because that is where our appetite finds nourishment and fulfillment while His spirit fights and rejects the unnecessary junk food that our flesh wishes to consume.

To the natural nature, God is invisible, and yet He is the only thing we can consume and feast on that will not leave us feeling empty. Our hunger for God's presence is how we are satisfied, because it is the only table that we can sit and feast at where the food never runs out or expires. We have often read in the book of Samuel about King David's love for God. King David was a man after God's own heart. His life weaved throughout the book of Psalm which often told of his search of God's presence no matter what situation he encountered. He was moved by what moved the heart of God. He wanted to know how God felt about life. He wanted to be intimately acquainted with God's ways of doing things and why He did them. He wanted to always remain passionate towards God. David was after God's heartbeat for the world. God's desire is that we pursue Him with all our heart as David did, abandoning ourselves to His purposes and plans.

How wonderful it is to chase after the heartbeat of God. God's heart is the one thing that we personally know that will not stop beating with a forever rhythm that keeps our hearts bouncing towards its everlasting beat.

The Heart of Worship

From the age of three I've always enjoyed worshipping and singing songs before the Lord. It delights my heart to please my Father. As an intercessor, worship serves as a passport that allows one's heart to go into a higher and deeper realm. One that often sits you in a seat before the Father's throne. Extolling Him for His greatness, His wisdom, His care, and His love. To call upon His name, to tell Him how great He is, just because He is who He is.

We must allow our worship to join in with our prayer life to increase and deepen our communion with God. Worship is all that we are, reacting rightly to all that He is, "The more we pray the more we should want to worship." Worshipping God allows our intercession time to call forth the Sovereign God who is able to do an abundant thing as His presence manifest in the life or situation we bring and lay down before His altar.

Before I ever learned what the true essence of prayer meant my heart was bent towards worship. We can see through scripture that God requires two things of Christians; to Pray and to Worship.

This is Personal

Again, the devil took him to a very high mountain, and showed him all the kingdoms of the world and the glory of them; and said to him, "All these I will give you, if you will fall down and worship me." Then Jesus said to him, "Begone, Satan! For it is written, "You shall worship the Lord your God and him only shall you serve." (Matthew 4:8-10)

Prayer and worship are matters of the heart and there must be an inner devotion on our part toward them both. Both are the outflow of what is already seeded in the heart. They go hand and hand; one is impossible to do without the other, they form an essential link and cannot be separated. When we worship, it strengthens and lifts our prayer's.

A person with a true heart of intercession will quite naturally find themselves slipping into worship, because both are fueled by the Holy Spirit and flow out of our spirit man. Prayer is a humble

This is Personal

conversation with God, and to be in the presence of God is to be aware of His holiness, which leads to worship. Worship brings forth our acknowledgment that only God is worthy and deserving of it.

It is essential to each category of Prayer. The Prayer of: Faith *(James 5:15)*, Agreement *(Acts 1:14)*, Supplication *(Philippians 4:6)*, Thanksgiving *(which is similar to worship only difference is worship focus on God himself and thanksgiving focuses on what God has done)*, Consecration *(setting a time apart to follow God's will Matthew 26:39)*, Intercession *(1 Timothy 2:1)* and Imprecation *(Psalms 7,55,69.)* Worship quickens our conscience and feeds our mind with the truth of God for effective prayer, which in turns brings a result of an even deeper worship. It also purges the imagination by allowing us to see the beauty of God, by opening the heart to the

This is Personal

love of God and prepares our devotion for the will and purpose of God.

Worship is not a feeling, but a posture an attitude expressed by one who knows that without God, we in turn are nothing. True worship is felt inwardly and expressed through our actions. The Apostle Paul said it like this, *"And so, dear brothers and sisters, I plead with you to give your bodies to God because of all he has done for you. Let them be a living and holy sacrifice the- kind he will find acceptable. This is truly the way to worship him. Don't copy the behavior and customs of this world, but let God transform you into a new person by changing the way you think. Then you will learn to know God's will for you, which is good and pleasing and perfect. (Romans 12:1-2)* Paul was basically saying, all of our humanness: our hearts, minds, hands, thoughts, attitudes are to be presented to God for His use. Although worship is often looked upon as

This is Personal

a command or a compliant to the demands of God, *"Our relationship with Him should Trump Command."*

As we live in relationship with God, we should find ourselves worshipping without even trying because it should be the foundation on which we are built. The command to worship obeys our relationship with Jesus Christ. Rather than always being in a petition mode, (requesting or asking) we must wisely shift our prayer direction occasionally. Not only does He honor the petitioner He also honors the worshipper. When we worship Him and let go of our own ideas, desires and agendas, we open ourselves up to connect with what is on His heart and we form a partnership with Him in what He wants to do. As an intercessor, there is always room to go deeper in God where there are no boundaries as we allow our

This is Personal

worship to lift-up our prayers to the Throne of God.

Examination

There are so many thoughts flowing through our minds. So many feelings and emotions flowing from our hearts that we must ask God to take a daily look within its chambers, to ensure that the things that are flowing through it will not be the very things that cause our prayers to be hindered. *Test me, Lord and try me, examine my heart and my mind. (Psalm 26:2)*

Our feelings and emotions often play a big factor in the way that we pray or if we even pray about something or not. Expressing emotion is a wonderful thing to do, but unless they are shaped by a mind saturated in truth, they can be destructive, and out-of-control forces. Where the mind goes, the will follows, and so do emotions.

This is Personal

First Corinthians 2:16 tells us *"we have the mind of Christ,"* not the emotions of Christ. We must remove our feelings from the process of prayer and replace it with the mind of Christ so that our prayers can become more effective here on earth. When we intercede on one's behalf, we should not allow our feelings to overshadow what God wants to do in their current situation. Praying with the mind of the Spirit will allow our heart and words to flow in accordance of His will. We must always honor God and look forwarded to the ways that we can release and remove barriers so He can deliver us from the things that weigh us down as we bow before His altar. What we bring forth and how we present ourselves shows the Father that we treasure Him. That He is our King and we have prepared ourselves for His service as our hearts desires to bring forth great reverence to His name. When every aspect of our being is in tune and aligned with His spirit it creates a charge in the atmosphere that produces miracles, healing, and deliverance.

Let's get to the center of things! Our hearts must match and line up with the Father's heart as we stated earlier. Prayer starts in the heart of God and prayers that agree with the will of God gets results. When we know God's heart for a situation, we can pray in agreement with His Spirit and expect His will to come to pass.

As an intercessor, you must realize that your prayers are not changing God's heart but in fact it's your heart that is changing to match God's will.

God can see things about you that no one else can see. Deep things. Hidden things. You know, those inner thoughts and desires that your family and friends have no idea are even drifting around in your heart and mind.

This is Personal

...but the Lord looks at the heart." 1 Samuel 16:7

Upon this land and living among this nation we have a plenty of people willing to work for a platform, recognition, and a chance to produce their own glory but few that are willing to do the work behind the scenes so that God is reflected instead of oneself. Prophets are the mouth of God, Missionaries are his feet, but Intercessors are His heart. We as intercessors must guard our hearts from offenses lest it corrupts us. When we start to take a deeper look at the inner chambers of our own hearts and start allowing God to peel away the layers, and remove the veil that cover our eyes; our spirit eyes can then begin to see that the picture of life advances further than ourselves. What we once saw through our physical eyesight will begin to look different because He has allowed us to see through His lens. Examination of one's self is a detailed

This is Personal

inspection that allows us the opportunity to evaluate, test and remove the unnecessary things that will keep us from fully preforming the way that God has created us to operate. There are a number of things that we as human beings have allowed to enter in our lives from the enemy or even our own hands, that has caused our prayer life to become dysfunctional and less effective, and until we allow the spirit of the Lord to examine and reveal to us what is conflicting our hearts, we will continue to live a life of inadequacy; one that is not operating and functioning at its full capacity.

Moses, as an intercessor for the people of Israel, constantly prayed for them, yet they complained and fought against him daily. At one point they wanted to even stone him. Sometimes the very people that we are interceding for will be the enemy's greatest tool against us so that we can stop

This is Personal

praying on their behalf and give up on them. He wants us to take in the offenses, so we can seek to destroy them by our words in prayer rather than lift them up before the altar. An intercessor's greatest gift is the love they hold in their heart for people through Jesus Christ.

It enables them to pray for love not hate, to save and not destroy, heal not kill, bless and not curse. Remember we have the greatest example that ever lived. Jesus hung on the cross as people mocked Him from below. Even the thief next to Him mocked His being, but Jesus *overcame the prosecution and betrayal through prayer, "Father forgive them; for they know not what they do..." (Luke 23:24)* Do not let your emotions, feelings, or even offenses keep you from praying and allowing love to be your greatest weapon.

Unconfessed sin- In our lives we must let go of sins that we have refused to confess before God. *"If I had cherished iniquity in my heart, the Lord would not have listened (Psalm 66:18)* Before we come to the conclusion that God does not want to listen or He just does not hear us, we must make sure that what we refuse to release is not the very thing that is keeping us separated from Him. We must admit our weaknesses and our failures before God. Honesty is the place where we receive healing. As we constantly confess all known sins and ask God to continue to reveal all unknown sins to us, we can grow closer to Him which will allow us to further build a relationship that aligns us with His will.

Unforgiveness- We have been forgiven for our offenses by the greatest of them all and somehow so often we have a hard time forgiving the ones who have hurt us. Sometimes people will insult, persecute and say all kinds of evil things against us, but forgiveness will always set us free. The

Bible tells us to *Leave your sacrifice there at the altar. Go and be reconciled to that person. Then come and offer your sacrifice to God. (Matthew 5:24)* Forgiveness is an important part to any kind of prayer. When we do not forgive others, our Father in heaven will not forgive our sins either. (Mark 11:25) Which will cause us to be separated from Him. As His child, it should be our desire to be as close to God as possible when praying and seeking His will, we cannot allow the enemy to tie us up with the chains of unforgiveness and yank on us every time we try to approach the throne of God with the guilt of unforgiveness buried in our hearts. We must release unforgiveness and chase after peace within ourselves and for others. As Jesus commanded Peter, "Put your sword away!" (John 18:11) There is a time and place as well as a different way to fight. The way we fight unforgiveness is to offer forgiveness to the offender even when it's not your fault.

Motives- Self check: what is fueling your desires? Is it selfish tendencies? It is a part of the human nature! Sometimes we regard our own interest ahead of the interest of others, and sadly we also regard our own interests ahead of God's will. *James 4:3 says, "And even when you ask, you don't get it because your motives are all wrong-you want only what will give you pleasure.*

Peter made a confession, *"You are the Christ, the Son of the living God."* *(Matthew16:16)*

But soon after Jesus told the disciples He must go to Jerusalem, be killed, and then raised from the dead. Peter responded, *"Far be it from you, Lord! This shall never happen to you" (Matthew 16:22)* Jesus said to Peter, Get behind me Satan. Why did

Jesus rebuke Peter the one who loved Him and served Him? It was because of his fleshly mindset. The things of man (Peter) got mixed into what he thought about the kingdom and how he pictured it to look like. He was blinded with his presumptions and his perspective, that he thought he could correct Christ.

How often in prayer do we love on Jesus but mistakenly mix in our genuine, Spirit-birth kingdom desires? If we are not careful, we can become manipulated by Satan, hindering our prayers, to advance the kingdom. Base what you pray for on verses from the Bible, claim God's promises using the words declared already in the Bible or words given to you from the leading of the Holy Spirit. When praying for yourself and others, you must deny yourself and ask only for the things that are consistent with the character and nature of God.

This is Personal

Nehemiah 1:5-11 gives a great example of a prayer that was based off God's promises, words, and works.

Unbelief – Sometimes when our prayers get stagnant, stuck, and seem like they are not being heard we may need to take another look at our faith. God wants us to have confidence in His ability and trust that He will provide what we need to attain Godliness. We must not pray from a place of rejection but from a place of expectancy.

"What do you mean, If you can? Jesus asked. "Anything is possible if a person believes." (Mark 9:23) Our God is able and capable of doing anything. What your natural mind may conceive as impossible our supernatural God is able to produce and conceive it to be possible. When you are lacking the understanding of God's timing and movement, do not allow it to cause your faith to become unbelief.

This is Personal

"If you need wisdom, ask our generous God, and he will give it to you. He will not rebuke you for asking. But when you ask him, be sure that your faith is in God alone. Do not waver, for a person with divided loyalty is as unsettled as a wave of the sea that is blown and tossed by the wind. Such people should not expect to receive anything from the Lord. (James 1:5-7)

Prayer and Faith must always be intertwining. When they work together, they bring forth the birthing of God's will to the earth.

Travailing; Birthing through Prayer

Earlier on most of my intercession prayers took place in the middle of the night. Awakened by the urging of the Holy Spirit to pray for different matters and different situations for people. Some by name of those I knew and other times names of people that would appear as a flash before

This is Personal

my eyes whom I was unfamiliar with. That may seem strange to you, but I never questioned I just prayed because someone's life depended on my willingness to yield to the Holy Spirit's leading.

"Always be Prepared, Ready to Pray, Ready to Labor, Ready to give birth."

One day as I was in my car driving, I felt an urge from the Holy Spirit to pray for a family member, as I began to call out his name in prayer, it felt different. It was like the air was dry and needed to be saturated by an outpour. As I continued to pray the miraculous happened, a quick rain shower came through and immediately, I heard the Spirit of the Lord say to me through a series of questions, you are praying for him and that is good, but does your heart weep for him? Do you feel the pain through the labor of the prayer? Will you weep for the heart of another? Are you willing to

This is Personal

birth someone else's breakthrough?" In that quick moment my heart was caught up with the beat of my Abba Father. My heart begun to weep for God to send His will through. Tears began to flow from my eyes and a groaning from my lips. The spirit of the Lord said I have called many to the ministry of prayer, to intercede. Many are praying but they are not crying out; they do not feel the break of my heart for my lost children. They say they love me, but they will not cry out and birth breakthrough for their sisters and brothers. To love me is to love them.

As intercessors, sometimes, we must labor before God in private on behalf of another. Not even speaking a public word about the labor pains we are feeling and experiencing on the behalf of someone else. Every prayer does not have to be publicized. God must have trust in you if He is going to allow the Holy Spirit to show

This is Personal

you things to pray about. So often our prayers are brought to death because we think the world and everything in it is our friend and they need to know what we are doing and who we are doing it for. We begin to release our prayers without guarding our words, and slowly but surely the enemy gets wind of what we are doing and hijacks our prayers because we need to be noticed. Sometimes it takes the silent tears of men and women passionately praying for souls to bring down the mercy of the Father for others.

"We have plenty of people willing to do work before man, but few that are willing to do work before the Lord."

I cried unto God with my voice, even unto God with my voice; and he gave ear unto me.

(Psalm 77:1kjv)

This is Personal

Travailing is a form of intense intercession given by the Holy Spirit whereby an individual is gripped by something that grips God's heart. The individual labors with Him for an opening to be created so that the new life can come forth. [Travail-give birth, hard work, the pains of childbirth, toiling, bring forth] Travailing takes place after you have carried something in your heart for a period, but it comes on you suddenly. The Holy Spirit wants to and comes to *bring forth.* John 7:38 says, *"From his innermost being shall flow rivers of living water"* Innermost being" is the word *koilia,* which means "womb." It has more to do with birthing something spiritually than what is happening to you as you do it in the physical. We are the womb of God on this earth. We are not the source of life, but we are carries of the source of life. We do not generate life, but we release it with our words in prayer from the Creator who does. Travailing can be associated with the flow of tears or even groaning. It is preceded by nurturing the promise. Later comes the push that promise has been born, and relief from the delivery is felt.

Sometimes, we must allow our hearts to weep for people that cannot weep for themselves. Hearts that are heavy laden, grieving for one reason or another. Maybe they have thrown in the towel, but God has not thrown them away.

We could never have the heart of God, but we could feel for a moment how He grieves for His children. As children of God we must allow the things that break the heart of God to break our heart. When the Kingdom is affected, we are affected. Just remember our weeping does not go unnoticed rather it is for ourselves or on another's behalf. Scripture says, *"that he gathers up all our tears and puts them in his bottle." (Psalms 56:8)* Although our prayer at times may bring on a sigh of weeping, we must believe that our tears will turn into shouts of joy even when we are crying out for others.

When Hagar lifted her voice in the wilderness of Beersheba, God drew near (Genesis 21:17) When Hannah wept bitterly outside the temple of the Lord, God noticed and remembered (1 Samuel 1:10, 17). When David became weary with moaning, God did not become weary with listening (Psalm 6:6-9)

Why did I mention these people you may ask? If you notice that when they cried out, travailed before God an opening of new birth came forth in their situation, God remembered, in fact, He drew near to them in their broken state and answered. I cannot repeat this enough, *"What breaks the heart of God should indeed break the heart of man."* When Mary fell apart at Jesus' feet over the death of her brother

This is Personal

Lazarus, scripture tells us that *Jesus wept* Jesus had compassion and wept- even though Jesus was about to speak a word to snatch Lazarus back from death. (John 11:43) The tears Christ wept for Lazarus were not tears of commiseration, but of displeasure and the stirring of His spirit.

Weeping so often is classified as a sign of weakness or even a sign of fear. However, weeping when joined with prayer in intercession testifies to God of the depth of our identity with those for whom we intercede. Intercession watered with your tears is one of the most powerful forms of prayer known. As surely as God is in heaven, *"Those who sow in tears will reap with songs of joy. He who goes out weeping, carrying seed to sow, will return with songs of joy, carrying sheaves with him." (Psalm 26:5-6)*

This is Personal

"Never look down on a person who sow in tears because it is the very thing that births their strength to carry the harvest."

"So I sought for a man among them who would make a wall, and stand in the gap before me on behalf of the land, that I should not destroy it; but I found no one"
Ezekiel 22:30

The nation of Israel was in a state of corruption and sin, God was looking for someone to stand in the gap, between Him and the land and cry out for deliverance.

The fact that God was looking for someone to stand in the gap shows us that it is His intention to respond to the cries of our hearts. We find in scripture that if we cry out to God it penetrates His heart and He answers. *"Call upon me in the day of trouble: I will deliver thee, and thou shalt glorify me." (Psalm 50:15)* Sometimes after many months or years of praying, a single

This is Personal

cry can bring direction or deliverance instantly.

Travailing can also be looked upon as wrestling. Wrestling in prayer enlists all the capacities of your soul, marshals your deepest holy desire and by the grace of God uses all the perseverance of your holy determination.

So, Jacob was left alone, and a man wrestled with him till daybreak. When the man saw that he could not overpower him, he touched the socket of Jacob's hip so that his hip was wrenched as he wrestled with the man. Then the man said, "Let me go, for it is daybreak." But Jacob replied, "I will not let you go unless you bless me." (Genesis 32:24-26)

Sometimes in prayer like Jacob tenacious, persevering prayer eventually pays off. Prayer is the source of life and power to see things change. Jacob knew the promises of God and held on until that breakthrough came forth even in the pain of His circumstances, He did not waiver from the possibility of change for the promise. Intercession involves taking hold of God's will and the refusal to let go of it until it comes to pass.

Prophetic Intercession

Have you ever felt burdened by a situation, hardly able to move past it, sensing and feeling the pains of another? As an intercessor, I have often experienced the urge of the Holy Spirit leading me to pray for others that are experiencing some type of pain in their body. I have also been prompted to pray about situations that I would not ordinarily know about.

For example, one night while asleep, I was awakened by the Holy Spirit with an excruciating pain in my stomach and suddenly I heard the Holy Spirit say,

"Cancer, Pray for your brother." I prayed all night until I felt the release of that burden. The next day my brother told me that he had visited the doctor due to a pain in his stomach and that he thought had the signs of cancer, but the report came back negative. Hallelujah! Praises be unto God! Confusing as this may seem to some, it feels quite natural to prophetic intercessors. I know that there are others that this may be happening to and they may not know how to handle it or the reasoning behind it. I thought that this area of intercession was worth mentioning and shining some light upon so others will know that this effect is not unusual at all.

*Prophetic Intercession: *the urge to pray, given by the Holy Spirit, for a situation or about a circumstance which you may have little natural knowledge about. But you are praying the prayer request that is on the heart of God.*

Prophetic intercessors love to pray and have a strong sense of intimacy when it comes to the Holy Spirit's leadings. In prayer they are well acquainted with the Holy Spirit's mysteries, burdens and travailing aspects when it comes to intercession. They also are given intuitive understanding concerning the situation they are praying about and maybe even the answer to the pray. They wait, listen, and read scriptures while letting the Holy Spirit remind them of the promise that is on His heart at that moment. It is the place where the priest and prophet unite, calling "for the earth to be filled with the knowledge of the glory of the Lord, as the water cover the sea" (Habakkuk 2:14).

Prophetic intercession is a ministry of faith, they are graced to pray for people and situations without knowing God's specific plans concerning the burden of prayer. Scripture says, *"the Spirit helps us in our weakness when we do not know what to pray for as we ought," (Romans 8:26)* As the Holy Spirit begins to pray through the intercessor's heart, they become the prayer-room of God Himself. The Spirit prays to the Father, and He who knows the mind of the Spirit heeds and acts according to what the Spirit prays, using them as the instrument.

As stated before, *Prayer begins with the ends of God.* He is the source in which we plug into and that is what in turn enables us to seek His power on behalf of others. While giving the intercessor (servant) the opportunity to stand in the gap for the weak and weary while receiving the rewards of intimacy with the Holy Spirit.

Anna

We have all heard about the story of Anna in the New Testament, which shows a slightly different side of a prophetic intercessor than I spoke about above, but brings forth more revelation to the ministry of a prophetic intercessor.

"Anna, a prophet, was also there in the Temple. She was the daughter of Phanuel from the tribe of Asher, and she was old. Her husband died when they had been married only seven years. Then she lived as a widow to the age of eighty-four. She never left the Temple but stayed there day and night, worshiping God with fasting and prayer. She came along just as Simeon was talking with Mary and Joseph, and she began praising God. She talked about the child to everyone who had been waiting expectantly for God to rescue Jerusalem." (Luke 2:36-38) Anna's primary assignment was to be in the temple. A woman of the secret place,

not praying before man but interceding and ministering before God. A holy and wise woman concentrating all her remaining years of energy on communing with God. A prophetess who saw the destiny of the small child Jesus when she held him in her arms (v.36). An intercessor who saw things that were not yet apparent to others (v.37). An evangelist who shared the Good News of the Messiah's arrival (v.38). Anna stayed faithful in her calling to long hours of prayer and fasting. She gives a great representation of what prophetic intercession is based around. Her calling transcends gender and age – young or old.

The foundational backing that gives accountability to this type of prophetic ministry can be easily identify through *Isaiah 62:6-7 "O Jerusalem, I have posted watchmen on your walls; they will pray day and night, continually. Take no rest, all you who pray to the Lord. Give the Lord no rest until he completes his work, until he makes Jerusalem the pride of the earth."*

This clearly emphasizes that God will raise up 24/7 prayer ministries in the end times, which will never be silent until Jesus returns. The promise of Isaiah 62:6-7 implies that some intercessors and ministries are called to engage in this as a full-time positioning. God's promise to appoint intercessors indicates that He will make a way for them to walk in this calling. Isaiah is referring to the New Testament believers. (Intercessors that will be on earth when Jesus returns) Isaiah and Ezekiel (Ezekiel 22:29-31) both spoke of a *spiritual wall* consisting of prayer. Intercessors are to make the wall by standing in the gap in prayer before God and the people, so that the land may be blessed rather than destroyed. Prophetic intercession, therefore, paves the way for the fulfillment of the prophetic promise.

Descriptions of a Prophetic Intercessor:

- They minster to God by declaring His worth unceasingly, reflecting the way He receives worship continually in heaven (Matthew 6:10).

- They wait to hear or receive God's word, His concerns, warnings, conditions, visions or promises in prayer.

- They labor-travail in intercession for the release of God's power to win the lost, bring revival to the body of Christ (the church), and impact the world. All while exhibiting compassion for His people.

- They mature (grow) in intimacy with God by the indwelling of the Holy Spirit, as it brings forth grace to love, obedience and partnership with Him.

- They gain the understanding of God's word, insight to His will, ways, and salvation.

This is Personal

When we serve God as intercessors, we are given grace to intercede and love to consume and spread. A mandate to serve others in prayer by allowing the Holy Spirit access to renew our mindset to think like Christ and permission to dwell in our being. The consistency of our obedience in prayer allows us to take the time and effort to grow in our understanding of God's word better, so we may help others understand God's heart and will for this time.

A prayer to have God's Heart

Father, in the mighty name of Jesus, help me to increase in spiritual awareness. Let the eyes of my heart be captivated by your love and awakened by your truths. I ask that you bring my heart into union with yours so we can form a partnership that will help me to bear the burdens and will in your heart. In

Prayer help me to look beyond the circumstances of the natural realm. Help me to see your Spirit at work and receive the Spirit of revelation and the authority to stand in the gap on the behalf of those I pray for. It is from your strength, through your might, and in your spirit oh Lord that I shall pray your prophetic promises into being. In Jesus' Name, Amen.

Faith is Required

Faith is birthed and stretched through our experiences with God. The more we seek and spend time with Him, the more our relationship with Him develops into a much deeper connection. *Hebrews 11:6 says, "And it is impossible to please God without faith. Anyone who wants to come to him must believe that God exists and that he rewards those who sincerely seek him,"*- and that is what we are doing when we pray. Many often struggle with this scripture because they wonder how can I pray in faith if I am not sure what I am praying for is in accordance to the will of God? The reasoning behind our struggle is that we have misplaced our faith. We believe that we must work our faith up to the place where God will honor our prayers, but in all reality, our faith should be based on God's power and not our imagination.

Faith is knowing that His abilities are not based on the capacity of our thoughts. He is God and He is Almighty. Nothing or no one can contend against Him and if we believe in Him then we believe that there is no limits that can sustain against His capabilities.

This is Personal

When it comes to intercession, faith and prayer are inseparable. Faith fuels prayer and Prayer expresses faith. The two should always be intertwined. One does not exist without the other. Faith is a knowledge within the heart beyond the reach of proof and prayer is the voice that lifts it up.

What does it mean to pray with Faith?

Faith and Prayer are a string of two cords, when we bind them together, they create a powerful twofold bond that cannot be easily broken. In prayer, they gracefully yield themselves apart for different situations called Assurance and Submission.

- Faith prays with Assurance- the act of being certain about something.

- Faith prays with Submission- the action or fact of accepting or yielding to the will or authority of another.

These two kinds of prayers are given to us for different situations and it is important to learn how to distinguish between the two.

Assurance

The essential principle of prayer is to know what you want; believe you will receive it according to God's will; visualize its arrival; and speak it into existence. This kind of confident prayer activates God's promises when His words are brought forth through prayer.

When we pray our assurance should be in the Lord; when prayer enters our hearts and exits our lips, they should speak the promises and blessing of God in faith.

Now faith is the confidence that what we hope for will actually happen; it gives us assurance about things we cannot see. (Hebrews 11:1)

This is Personal

Let's examine the life of Elijah, he was a man just like us who prayed earnestly in his time and day. A land where a great deal of idolatry was taking place and people were worshipping Baal. He prophesied that it would not rain and as he spoke forth it did not rain on the land for three and a half years.

Elijah must have been sure that what he spoke forth, would happen because 1 Kings tells us that he went into the court of tyrant, King Ahab and said, *"As surely as the Lord, the God of Israel, lives, the God I serve, there will be no dew or rain during the next few years until I give the word!" (Kings 17:1)* You must know that Elijah had to be absolutely sure that the answer to his prayer was in order with God's will to speak to a King in that time. Elijah not only spoke and prayed with assurance he also prayed in submission. He spoke knowing that his dependency was on God. To be sure that your prayers are in accordance to God's will, you can ask yourself these questions regularly.

- Do my words in prayer resemble or reflect the character of God in scripture?

- Is it according to the principles of the Christian life?

- Does my request in prayer glorify God?

- Does the Holy Spirit give me freedom to ask the request that I have petitioned?

God desires that His children live in joy, not despair; assurance, not anxiety; and boldness, not fear. When our prayers are according to His will God will give us the ability to bear down in prayer and speak with assurance, so when we pray it will be heard and the answer will be yes because it is in accordance to His will.

This is Personal

Submission

After Elijah's first confrontation with King Ahab, God sent him to the Kerith Brook. There Elijah sat with no food and no provisions. But God saw and knew his needs. It was there in a place of having nothing that God sent ravens to bring him food.

So he did what the Lord had told him. He went to the Kerith Ravine, east of the Jordan, and stayed there. The ravens brought him bread and meat in the morning and bread and meat in the evening, and he drank from the brook. (1Kings 17:5-6)

At this time Elijah was in hiding from King Ahab, he had no way to meet his needs. He was at the complete mercy of God Himself. As he continued to walk in obedience, God provided for His servant. Elijah did not fear when his provisions dried up. He knew full well that God was faithful and would always be unfailing to those who serve Him.

Some people slowly give God access to enter into their hearts, and some people give Him access right away. Just know He will never bulldoze His way in and will never force you to be obedient or submissive. He simply knocks and quietly waits to be invited in as you grant Him the access to use you as a yielded vessel. When praying in submission and keeping in step of obedience we can come to God with a bold voice and a humble heart with our request and He will faithfully provide.

Prayer of Submission

Lord, help me overcome my selfish desires in prayer, so that I may experience a fully activated prayer life that will bring forth your glory with my words. Help me to identify any areas in my life that have not yielded fully to your control. You are my

Lord and Savior everything I need comes from you and you are enough. Lord, help me to know and submit to your perfect will, so that my desires of being on top, in charge, or in control will take a back seat to your will. Lord, I realize the only way to be lifted up by you is to bow before you in submission. Cleanse me, refine me, stand up in me when I pray your words. In Jesus' name, authority and power will soar upward as the mighty wind. Amen

Boldness

The key to being bold and confident in prayer is to trust in the Father, and that comes from entering His presence to be with Him, not just to get something. He knows each of us intimately and is eager for us to know His heart. And as we spend time with God, we will also discover what He wills for our lives and situations.

At the usual time for offering the evening sacrifice, Elijah the prophet walked up to the altar and prayed, "O Lord, God of Abraham, Isaac, and Jacob, prove today that you are the God of Israel and that I am your servant. Prove that I have done all this at your command. O Lord, answer me! Answer me so these people will know that you, O Lord, are God and that you have brought them back to yourself. (1Kings 18:36-37)

Elijah spoke and prayed with boldness. He asked in faith trusting and believing that God was able and willing to answer his prayers. He was in complete tune with God which allowed him to hear from God. He prayed in agreement with what God asked of him, and without fail as servants and believers we can ask the same of God, with Elijah as an example, God can exceed our expectation and fulfill our expectancy in His timing.

Faith and God's Timing

By observing the life of Elijah, we see how God honors the word brought forth from the servant mouth. One reason we give up so often on prayer is because it seems pointless: in our minds, nothing has changed. However, what we cannot see is the Lord's activity behind the scenes. Sometimes He is readying the circumstances before He sends an answer. Often, He is preparing us to receive what He wants to provide. As we become more aware of God's character and nature, we will begin to understand that God's timing is not our timing. Elijah understood that all answers do not come immediately. He knew that we must remain persistent in prayer until we see a breakthrough. He prayed the drought in existence and petitioned God to bring the rain.

Many of us have prayed for many years about certain things, a lost family member,

This is Personal

a broken marriage, a career change, a desire, dream, or maybe for God to bring revival to the land. Whatever God has laid on your heart to pray, perhaps you have not seen the fulfillment of those prayers just yet. You still believe that God will bring forth the manifestation of that prayer to the land. Here is what I tell you, hello intercessor, there is preparation in the process of prayer. God has His way of getting us ready for the answer. He stretches our faith while revealing what is in our hearts.

At the very beginning of my call, which I am sure that others would agree, I was impatient, anxious, and perhaps even restless until God stepped in and crucified my flesh, purified me, and helped me to get ready so that when He released the answer I could handle it in the right way. God is not building His kingdom in the flesh or through the influence of man, but He is building it with faith and that involves praying, trusting, and moving in His timing in His way. God will act if you do not give up, He sees what you think is a crisis and He stands and says I have already prepared the way. He is concerned and the answer will be delivered at the right time.

Prophetic Note- Even as I am writing this book, I see in the spirit bricks being placed on top of bricks. Each one of them making the others solid and stronger. The spirit of the living God says, I am building you intercessor, stay the course do not give up. I am God and in this time and moment I am building you, preparing you for the rain. Yes, you are the one I have called and elected to do a great work.

Delayed not Denied

Whether it is a family member you are praying for or a vision that God has given you, be patient. Scripture says, *"But do not overlook this fact, beloved, that with the Lord one day is a thousand years, and a thousand years as one day. The Lord is not slow to fulfill his promise as some count slowness but is patient toward you..." (2 Peter 3:8-9)* The clock on the wall does not resemble His movement. *"For still the vision awaits it appointed time; it hastens to the end- it will not lie. If it seems slow, wait for it, it will surely come; it will not delay. (Habakkuk 2:3)* Intercessor I encourage you to stay in the process of prayer until the answer comes. *"but as for me, I will look to the Lord; I will wait for the God of my salvation; my God will hear me." (Micah 7:7)*

Sometimes we must simply wait. Scripture advises us to *Be still and know that he is God*, because if we chose to run ahead of Him, we may cause harm to ourselves or even our own demise. There are two necessary elements we should have in waiting:

This is Personal

- A complete dependence on God.

- Willingness to allow God to decide the terms, including the timing of His plans.

The word "wait" in the Bible carries the idea of confident expectation and hope. "For God alone my soul waits in silence... my hope is from him." (Psalm 62:1,5) To wait upon the Lord is to except something from Him in Godly hope, and the hope of the Lord does not disappoint! (Romans 5:5) That does not mean we should sit idly by as we wait on the Lord to act on our behalf. We should not spend our time doing nothing, rather, we should continue to do the work He has given us to do. *Psalm 123:2 says, "As the eyes of slaves look to the hand of their master, as the eyes of a female slave look to the hand of her mistress, so our eyes look to the Lord our God, till he shows us his mercy."* We should look to God with anticipation and willingness to serve as a servant shows to His master.

The idea of waiting on the Lord is not so much like a patient in the waiting room of the doctor's office, but like a waiter working in a restaurant. In a doctor's office they are seated and waiting to be call with no work or effort being made. In a restaurant the waiter is expecting the arrival of guests and upon entry of the guests, the waiter waits on them by serving them. As intercessors our waiting is serving in prayer as we await the coming of the promises of God. Our attitude and actions should be as those of a waiter anticipating (God's Word to manifest) and meeting the requests of the one we are praying to (Ministering before God). It is filling our time with service to the Master, always on our feet, ready, attentive to minister as the intimation of what He wants us to pray about comes about.

This is Personal

Scripture also references us to be still, which means we have ceased from following our own agenda or ingenuity. We have stopped trusting in our own strength and will power.

Trusting God's timing is sometimes hard for the human mind to grasp but God's wisdom far exceeds our own. As we come to God with our specific requests, He promises that our prayers are not in vain, even if we do not receive specifically what we ask for, we must remember He grants the things that are in accordance with His will. Sometimes what we are asking God for may not be in His timing for our current situation, or maybe we are at a place in our lives where we are not mature enough to handle what we are petitioning God for. A Father knows best for His child and our heavenly Father answers according to His wisdom and for our benefit. In these situations, we are to be diligent and persistent in prayer, but not always voicing our wants but also allowing Him to speak back to us in prayer with His concerns. Remember that prayer should not be our means of getting God to do our will on earth, but rather as a means of getting God's will done on earth. Even in prayer *you must trust in the Lord with all your heart and lean not on your own understanding; in all your ways submit to him, and he will make your paths straight. (Proverbs 3:5)* God is full of wisdom; nothing of knowledge lies outside of Him; He knows best and does all things well when it comes to our needs and the essence of our being. The patience to wait is not of the human nature; our flesh wants nothing but to pursue things in its on timing and seek out it's desires. *(The microwave mentality: push a button and have your answer in minutes)*

This is Personal

Psalm 40 tells us David waited patiently for the Lord to respond to his prayer. Patience is a fruit of the spirit. *(Galatians 5:22-23)* It is also a supernatural gift given by a supernatural God to His children that comes along with the filling of His spirit. It is not in our nature as human beings to wait but the spirit waits and purse the things of the spirit of God when He is ready to release His will for our good. God is faithful to us even when we are not faithful to ourselves. He does not allow destruction to come upon us when we trust that He knows best. We must keep praying, keep serving, keep believing and keep trusting that the answer is on the way.

"Do not throw away your confidence; it will be richly rewarded. You need to preserve so that when you have done the will of God, you will receive what he has promised. (Hebrews 10:35-36)

This is Personal

Prophetic Note- For the vision awaits its appointed time; it hastens to the end- it will not lie. If it seems slow, wait for it; it will surely come; it will not delay. Even now I hear the spirit of the Lord saying, "Intercessor be of courage; All of heaven has heard your cry. Your tears and prayers have not gone unnoticed. The Father who sits high and looks low has been attentive towards his servant. Your faithfulness has been seen by His eyes and your tears have reached heaven's door, for I am not slow to fulfill my promises says the Lord as some count slowness for I the Lord Almighty have opened the heavens above and released your answer. The delay is over. "Prayer is not a preparation for the battle; It is the battle."

When we live in the flesh, we often want to fix things in the flesh. Our minds and hearts are filled with questions:

This is Personal

What more can I do? What should I do? What do I need to do? As we continue to pray, we must never forget what Ephesians 6:13 says,

For our struggle is not against flesh and blood, but against the rulers, against the authorities, against the powers of this dark world and against the spiritual forces of evil in heavenly realms.

This is Personal

3 The Intercessors Battlefield

Often when things are going great and it looks like we are in the clear and nothing can go wrong. We start to relax and become comfortable in our space. Then out of nowhere comes sickness, disease, financial setbacks, mood swings, problems in marriage, issues with children, oppression, depression and a host of other things trying to bring you to a demise.

Welcome to the battlefield, where the enemy never quits, and prayer never ceases. Being in war is not an option. Whether you engage in battle or choose to sit or even run, Satan and his troops are coming to attempt to try and stop what God has planned.

As intercessors we must allow the commander and chief to navigate us through the battlefield, He has the

This is Personal

authority and the proper credentials to lead us to victory. He has forehand knowledge on the enemy's whereabouts, strategies, tactics and plans.

God says stand up and know your authority through me and use it. God does not teach us to pray or fight from a position of weakness, but a position of strength through Jesus Christ.

On the battlefield while we are on our knees in prayer, God is fighting and moving before us. Strengthening, helping, and upholding us with His victorious right hand.

Know Your Enemy

It is so important for the intercessor to understand who and what they are fighting against on the battlefield. The key to God's plan for our lives is prayer, but the battleground is not of this earth. The fight takes place in the spiritual realm, where we battle against the prince of this world and his agents for our lives, our families, our friends, and our nation. Unfortunately, we are sometimes unaware and misinformed about Satan and his army. Our lack of spiritual knowledge allows our minds to form a fear of his name alone. Anytime his name comes up in the bible or in simple conversation we want to speed right pass and not show a care to who he is and what he is about. The one thing about engaging in war is you cannot fight against something or someone you have no knowledge about. How will you prepare and strategize? How will you stay ready for war? Prayer alone is powerful but in warfare it is not enough, you must know your target. I am not saying we should be consumed with learning about Satan because no one can contend against God. What I am saying is that Satan knows a great deal about us and we in turn should know about him.

This is Personal

For we are not fighting against flesh-and-blood enemies, but against evil rulers and authorities of the unseen world, against mighty powers in this dark world, and against evil spirits in the heavenly places. (Ephesians 6:12)

What looks like flesh and blood (people/circumstances) when we are attacked in the natural are only tools used by the enemy, but they should not be our target in prayer. They are really an effect of a spiritual battle taking place in the heavenly realms. Did you know that there are three heavens? Growing up in a Baptist and religious church as a young girl, they never really explained or talked much about the three different heavens. It was not until I was an adult pursuing my love for Jesus, that I learned about the different heavenly realms. I know if it took me that long to learn then there are probably others who are also still experiencing this

This is Personal

lack of spiritual knowledge even as they are reading this. First, let me share the foundation scripture to back what needs to be recognized. *In the beginning God created the heavens and the earth. (Genesis 1:1)* Take notice the "s" on heaven in this verse. Which indicates that there is more than one heaven that exists. Also, Hebrews 7:26, *which says that Jesus, our High Priest, is "exalted above the heavens"*; in other words, Jesus is in a heaven beyond other heavens. Below I have listed some basic 101 knowledge about the three heavens.

- 1st Heaven- The natural atmosphere that surrounds the earth. The air that we breathe. The realm that the birds and the clouds reside. *(Genesis 1:20) Then, God said, "Let the waters swarm with fish and other life. Let the skies be filled with birds of every kind." The natural atmosphere that surrounds the earth.*

- 2nd Heaven- Outer space; the place where the stars and planets reside. The realm in which demonic spirits operate. *(Ephesians 6:12) For we are not fighting against flesh- and- blood enemies, but against evil rulers and authorities of the unseen world, against mighty powers in this dark world, and against evil spirits in the heavenly places.*

- 3rd Heaven- The heaven in which God lives. *(2 Corinthians 12:2) Apostle Paul states, "I was caught up to the third heaven fourteen years ago. Whether I was in my body or out of my body, I don't know- only God knows. (Ephesians 1:20-23) That raised Christ from the dead and seated him in the place of honor at God's right hand in heavenly realms. Now he is far above any ruler or authority or power or leader or anything else- not only in this world but also in the world to come. God has put all things under the authority of Christ and has made him head over all things for the benefit of the church.*

In our prayers/intercession we must realize that just like there are different heavenly realms, not all situations, warfare or demonic forces are fought on the same level. There are also three different ranks of spiritual forces working around us.

- Ground level – (Luke 10:17-20) This level is most common in our lives. It wages war against our repentance and salvation. This is the level which casting out demons often takes place. This was the most common type of demonic encounter that took place when Jesus walked the earth. Intercessors can engage in this level by their right standing, faith and maturity in relationship with God.

- Occult level- (2 Corinthians 10:3-5) This level is when demons are activated against us through word curses. This could be brought on by bitterness (Ephesians 4:26-27), unforgiveness, Sin (John 8:34), rebellion (1 Samuel 15:23) and pride. The heart and mind is the head of this battleground of warfare and the tongue is the weapon. On this level,

This is Personal

intercessors pray to release God's word and blessings in order to set people free.

- Territorial level- (Daniel 10, Mark 5:10) Geographical, neighborhoods, cites, counties, regions states and nations. This is the level where intercessors engage in war against principalities and powers that directly influence and control lives in that region politically and religiously. This level of war is usually dealt with by many intercessors and armies of saints.

When in battle, we must pray beyond our physical awareness and pray from a place of our spiritual senses, so we are not fighting against the wrong enemy as Satan would like us to do.

If we are not carful our intercession can be ineffective or counterproductive because of our failure to understand our positioning in prayer. Prayerfully the above revelation will help you understand that your intercession and spiritual engagement must be initiated and sustained from the third heaven. It is from there we receive the revelation that we need to fight in the first and second heaven. When it comes to intercession, our knowledge on the things of God can be one of our greatest weapons. When we are called and instructed by the Holy Spirit to engage in spiritual warfare through intercessory prayer we must be knowledgeable, trained, accountable and under a covering for our mere protection. Through God's wisdom we are given the tools, strategy and the ultimate reward in prayer which is victory.

Discernment

The purpose of discernment for a believer, especially an intercessor, is to know the spirit by the spirit and to see their activities and operations at any given time. Discernment allows believers to effectively take authority over demonic

This is Personal

activity in warfare. It is not for fascination, fear or head knowledge. Discernment is given as an awareness mechanism. *Look, I have given you authority over all the power of the enemy, and you can walk among snakes and scorpions and crush them. Nothing will injure you.* (Luke10:19). The realm of the spirit is a dangerous realm and must not be entered in casually, but with wisdom. Intercessors should not pray with eyes closed in hopes or attempts to hit their target. Our intercessions should be done strategically, on point and on target. God relies on the activities of the intercessor to do what He wills to do because it enforces the Kingdom of God on earth. Intercessors must be willing and prepared. It is so important as you intercede and stand in the gap for others that you pray to keep a pure heart. The Holy Spirit will give you discernment needed for the call and a watchmen's eye to see as you stand on the wall. The enemy does not care who you are he goes after whatever stands in his way as soon as the door is left open.

As Peter wrote in 1 Peter 5:8 *"Stay alert! Watch out for your great enemy, the devil. He prowls around like a roaring lion, looking for someone to devour."*

I remember not too long ago a geographic special came on about lions. One part of the episode featured the way they hunted prey. As they looked upon their prey, I noticed how they ran after the weak ones that did not stay in step with the group. From the looks of it they knew if they kept in pursuit of the one that lagged, looked confused and weak they had their catch.

That is a lot like what he tries to do with us as Christians. When we seem to be weak and left to run for ourselves and we do not stay in the step of the spirit, and we get devoured.

This is Personal

The Bible tells us *"in the same way, prayer is essential in this ongoing warfare. Pray hard and long. Pray for your brothers and sisters. Keep your eyes open. Keep each other's spirits up so that no one falls behind or drops out. (Ephesians 6:18 msg)*

The enemy has planned and plotted against you and others since the day you entered your mother's womb. Studying and learning what makes you vulnerable and weak. He has had time to scheme against your life. Yes, he has a well thought out plan to accomplish *John 10:10 "The thief's purpose is to steal and kill and destroy...*

Jesus warned against this in John 16:33 *"I have told you all this so that you may have peace in me. Here on earth you will have many trials and sorrows. But take heart, because I have overcome the world."*

"Intercessors do not pray for victory, but from a place of victory. Prayer is about position and posture."

We know that by the power of the cross, Satan has been stripped of his power, shamed and subdued. So, if he is defeated and it is done then why must we still fight in prayer? Although his defeat is absolute, it must be appropriated.

Picture it like this, was Jesus death for sin absolute? Yes. He was the propitiation for our sins, and not for our sins only but for the whole world (1 John 2:2). Is the whole world saved? No. Salvation is only good for those who appropriate it. If you do not claim it, it will not do you any good. He that believeth not is condemned already (John 3:18) so we must appropriate what has already been done through the work of Jesus Christ at the cross and through the salvation that He has given. The victory in our prayers is from our position in Christ

This is Personal

(relationship) not from our words. *Ephesians 2:6 says, "For he raised us from the dead along with Christ and seated us with him in the heavenly realms because we are untied with Christ Jesus.* Rather than praying from earth to heaven we must pray from heaven to earth.

The seven sons of Sceva learned a lesson from this very thing you are reading about now. Claiming they could cast out demons, but did not personally know the Lord. As they came upon a demon possessed man and commanded, in the name of Jesus whom Paul preaches (secondhand religion), come out of him. That man turned and stripped them of their clothing and begun to beat them. They fled wounded and naked. They were trying to take authority over the devil but did not have the proper relationship with Jesus to do such a task. When we come up against the devil and his army even as a child of

God it must be from a position of personal relationship with Jesus Christ.

Our relationship and seated position in Christ allows us to be enthroned with the Lord, when He died, you died. When He rose, you rose. When He ascended, you ascended. When He took His seat at the right hand of the Father, you are in Him, and seated with Him.

Dressed for Battle

In the military regardless of what branch you are in there is a special unique attire worn in the time of battle. The same is true for Christian soldiers as well. We have a uniform for the kingdom that protects us from our enemies.

Engaging in spiritual warfare is not a game and should not be taken lightly. When we go in battle for ourselves and others, we must be fully prepared to protect

This is Personal

ourselves from the fiery arrows of the devil. Like any other war when we are not fully covered there could be a result of casualty of war.

As Paul *Ephesians 6:10-19* says, *"A final word: Be strong in the Lord and in his mighty power. Put on all of God's armor so that you will be able to stand firm against all strategies of the devil...*

Therefore, put on every piece of God's armor so you will be able to resist the enemy in the time of evil. Then after the battle you will still be standing firm. Stand your ground, putting on the belt of truth and the body armor of God's righteousness. For shoes, put on the peace that comes from the Good News so that you will be fully prepared. In addition to all of these, hold up the shield of faith to stop the fiery arrows of the devil. Put on salvation as your helmet, and take the sword of the Spirit, which is the word of God.

This is Personal

Pray in the Spirit at all times and on every occasion. Stay alert and be persistent in your prayers for all believers everywhere. And pray for me, too. Ask God to give me the right words so I can boldly explain God's mysterious plan that the Good News is for Jews and Gentiles alike.

Wearing defective, flawed or cracked armor can cause you to be injured when you are in prayer. The armor of God serves as a protection for His people so we must daily examine it and give it the necessary maintenance to keep it in tack. You cannot afford to walk out on the battlefield alone (without God) or with dysfunctional armor, it is a recipe made for disaster. Satan is observing and looking for any cracks within your armor to destroy and kill whatever you are praying for before it ever leaves your heart and forms on your lips.

When we follow Jesus and answer His call, it draws us into a spiritual battle because the devil realizes that he has lost a soul. Fortunately, for us God has already prepared a safety mechanism for this type of backlash. God is faithful, he did not forsake us or leave us defenseless against the attacks of the enemy. He has equipped us and provided the necessary protective gear to keep us from folding in the heat of pursuit while we are in prayer and under His Lordship.

As we go forward let us begin to take a deeper look at our armor and speak and declare words that can keep it at its best performance. If we plan on surviving while interceding on the behalf of others, then we must understand the nature and purpose of each piece of armor and implement it in battle.

This may go without saying but always know that God is in control. He is the ruler over all forces and when He takes command your armor is covered by His hands as He allows you to pull down strongholds in the spiritual realm.

- **The Belt of Truth-** Represents freedom in movement against the enemy. It is not surprising that the belt of truth is mentioned first. Truth is the utmost importance in the life of a Christian. *John 14:6, "declares that Jesus is the way the truth and the life"* Truth must rule in the heart of an intercessor, be a part of their mindset and be declared off of their lips daily.
- **The Breastplate of Righteousness-** Protects the heart; also provides protection against the unexpected. In the heat of battle there may be blows that come from unexpected directions or there could be more than one enemy to ward off. The breast plate protects everything on which the intercessor is spiritual existence

depends on. *Apart from Christ there is no righteousness, but through Jesus you have been "born again" and made righteous in His sight.*

- **With Feet Fitted with the Readiness that comes from the Gospel of Peace-** Without a solid footing, the enemy is sure to bring even the best soldier down. We must be assured by our standing in God because our feet represent victory. (Romans16:20) *May I reflect the gospel in my words and action, that through me, my encounter with others may draw them one step closer to God.*
- **The Shield of Faith-** Shields were used both to push against the enemy and block the blows and fiery arrows of the enemy. In prayer we must declare: *We take God at His word and His promises are true, everlasting, and abundant.*
- **The Helmet of Salvation-** The helmet protects the head and mind. As an intercessor if your mind is not in proper functioning properly, then you will not be able to fight. *The helmet gives us a constant reminder that nothing can separate us from*

This is Personal

His unfailing love and that we have been saved by grace and our salvation is maintained in Christ.

- Sword of the Spirit- The Word; Rhema of God. This is the only offensive weapon mentioned. *"For the word of God is alive and powerful. It is sharper than the sharpest two-edged sword, cutting between soul and spirit, between joint and marrow. It exposes our innermost thoughts and desire (Hebrews 4:12)."* Lord, help us as intercessors to be filled with the Holy Spirit and may your word be buried in our hearts that we are able to bring forth what you have spoken in your words

*The posture of Prayer- This one is not so much a weapon, but the method to engage our weapons against the enemy. It is not said to be a part of the armor, but it seems to be a part of what keeps it in tack and firmly fitted. So, I cannot let it go without mentioning. *As we pray in the spirit on all occasions Lord help us to be alert and always praying for the saints and* *intercessor in the land. Help us be thankful and joyful through our surrendered prayers.*

Loaded and Locked

Prayer is the battlefield, the armor of God is our attire, and the Word of God is our weapon. Loaded, locked, properly trained and ready to engage. Knowing the word of God as an intercessor is the most valuable weapon, we can possess because it brings forth truth. Scriptures, the inspired word of God, that is brought forth by the way of the Bible is the *thought* of God expressed. Scripture tells us that God's thoughts are higher than our thoughts. It tells of God's promises and serves as an instruction manual giving us direction on how to stand firm. It works as both an offense and defense weapon.

What an amazing power we have been given to fight the devil's lies. It is the

This is Personal

reason why Satan fights so hard against us because if we properly took hold of the authority of God's word, it would be so detrimental to him and his army. If you do not know the truth you cannot possibly recognize a lie, right? *Hosea 4:6 says, "My people are destroyed for a lack of knowledge..."*. Truth is vital to an intercessor engaging in battle, because knowing the truth will stop the attacks of the enemy in which he launches against our mind. God's word brings on knowledge, but what good is scripture if we do not use the tool in which it was created. The word of God is at your disposal, take hold of it, it speaks, it aims, and it launches. We must stop giving the devil more credit than he deserves. If we allow him to influence and have control over our lives and build him up greater than who he is, our prayers would be worthless, wasteful and useless because

This is Personal

we have placed him above The Almighty God.

Watch and Stand Your Post

Be aware and alert that at every moment you are on call. Being called to the ministry of intercession is like being a doctor who carries a pager. At any given moment you can be called for an emergency. Whatever you are doing and no matter where you are the Holy Spirit may call you to change your plans, pray and sound the alarm to stop the enemy's attack. Truth is the enemy is never going to alert you when he is ready to engage you in war. It is our responsibility to stand on our post and watch. We must never be caught off guard that is why the Bible commands us to gergoreuo and agrupneo (Greek word meaning watch, stay awake and be sleepless.) They are usually meant in the metaphorical and spiritual sense, to be vigilant and on guard, fully awake, aware, alert and focused. When we look at Matthew 26:37-40 we see that Jesus is talking about the disciples physically watching but as we continue to read, Matthew 26:41 it opens up a more spiritual depth, *"Keep watch and pray, so that you will not give in to temptation. For the spirit is willing [good intentions], but the body [human willpower] is weak."*

That is why in life prayer must be a lifestyle. When I looked up the words life and lifestyle in the Webster dictionary it states life means time and lifestyle which is a way in which a person lives. In other words, a manner in which you use your time towards doing something a certain way and it has become part of your norm no matter where you are or what you are doing your heart, mind and spirit are always ready to engage in it at any given time because it is in an eternal posture.

Be very careful, then, how you should live-not as unwise but as wise, making the most of every opportunity, because the days are evil. Therefore do not be foolish, but understand what the Lord's will is. (Ephesians 5:15-17) In pray is where an intercessor will find the will of God. In this place His will, will establish our lifestyles.

Get Set, Ready, Go

When I was in high school, I was a part of my high school track team. I ran the four by one relay where there were four runners at each 100 meter mark [on post in their lane] ready to receive [what God truths brings] the baton to run [pray] their part as fast as they could [bring forth]. Had you not been on post, focused on your lane, set and ready to take the baton when the runner approached [the word] you would

This is Personal

not have the best opportunity to get off to a good [strong] start and get to your mark quicker and smoother than the other runners. [Ahead of the enemy to see his next move] This experience also helped me to realize that I am not the only runner [Intercessor] trying to get to the finish line. It takes a team and we are only one part of the Body of Christ. Sometimes we must run on when one can no longer run for themselves. Intercession is just like that when other laborers get weary, we must take the baton and keep praying. Praying that God will give them strength to get back up again. *Matthew 9:37 says, "He said to his disciples, "The harvest is great, but the workers are few." We are made strong in numbers!* We must pray that God will send the workers, other intercessors to take the baton and arise to the occasion of prayer.

We must stand at our appointed posts on high alert waiting for the Holy Spirit's

This is Personal

nudging or God's voice to call us into prayer. Withdrawing from distractions, as Jesus did when He withdrew before dawn to an isolated location. (Mark 1:35) Going away as Jesus went away and remaining on our post to hear the Father's voice by shutting down all internal noises, simply watching, listening and waiting on what God wants to say. Just like our great intercessor Jesus did, we as earthly intercessors should do this, once we hear something [watch], we should do something [pray] – write it down, pray from it, and be ready to sound the alarm [call out and warn].

The Prophet Habakkuk:

"I will stand at my watch and station myself on the watchtower; and I will keep watch to see what he will say to me, and what I will answer when I am reproved. And the Lord answered me: Write the vision, and make it plain on tablets, that he who reads it may

run. For the vision is yet for an appointed time; but it speaks of the end, and does not lie. If it delays, wait for it; it will surely come, it will not delay." (Hab.2:1-3)

As God is our commander and chief and we must make sure that we are moving by His spirit. The Holy Spirit reveals to intercessors the intimate needs of those whom we intercede on the behalf of. There is a proper time and place to sound the alarm. The things God shares with us are not to be told to others unless He condones its release. This is a precious trust that He has released to His servant and we have to honor it as such.

This is Personal

For us to reach the pinnacle of Godly success, it is a must that we keep God at the forefront of our plans.

"Study this Book of Instruction continually. Meditate on it day and night so you will be sure to obey everything written in it. Only then will you prosper and succeed in all you do." (Joshua 1:8)

This is Personal

4 Breaking Barriers

Walking before God with a pure heart is the intercessor's motto. Keeping our hearts pure helps us to properly discern areas in which God wants us to pray. A couple of years ago I was invited to a class that was entitled *Building a Relationship with God through Prayer.* The leader asked each attendee to share a time when they thought that their prayer life lacked or a reason why it seemed to lack at that moment. One attendee said that there were days they get swamped with work and when they finally get home to pray, they have no energy or their homelife requires a lot of their remaining time.

In the previous chapter we discussed spiritual warfare and how we must be aware of our enemy. The enemy takes great honor and pride in his work to steal our purpose, destroy our call, and kill our destiny. He plans, strategizes and plots on ways he can keep us busy and wear us out. Which often leaves us feeling to tried to pray, guilty over our lack of communion with God and ultimately silencing our voice. Satan's mission is to snatch our investment in prayer to make us think that our deposit into it is no longer valued or effective. He seeks to put a lid on our prayers, while clutching them to the bottom of the barrel with his lies and claims.

I have learned in this Christian walk that what you value you will treasure. An intercessor should value truth and their time in the presence of God. No matter what you are going through if you value your communion with the Father, you will do it. Even if that meant that you had to climb over mountains and break lids to hear God's voice you would pursue it.

This is Personal

Sometimes the struggle is real, but God knows all about it. Our hobbies, our jobs, and even our families should take second place to our Creator. He is the maker of all things. Nothing is made, orchestrated or possessed without His knowledge. He knows our flaws and rescues us from our struggles. He has built you for the assignment and He has made a way for you to remove every barrier designed to stop you from accomplishing it.

Fasting

"The need is great, but our God is greater." You've commanded, rebuked, and prayed prayers. But there is no change. Sometimes you have to do something unusual for something extraordinary to happen.

I remember before I got saved my marriage was on the rocks, my job seemed to take all my time from my children and I lack greatly in my relationship with God. I

This is Personal

got to a point where I was just existing and not living out my God purposed life. I knew that prayer wasn't going to be enough to break the cycle I was experiencing. I remember one day I woke up and declared over my life that enough was enough. I was no longer going another day without feeling God's presence, lack in my marriage and depriving my children of my time and love due to my job. However, I knew I couldn't do it in my own strength. I needed a move of God to break the chains that was keeping me confined in brokenness. I was determined if I was going to be broken it wasn't going to be by the hands of the enemy. I needed to be emptied to make room for what I expected God to do on my behalf. That day I fasted (which I had never done before) and prayed and believe in God for the healing in the areas I felt needed his touch the most. That very night I attend church and was saved with the evidence of speaking in tongues. I was freed and left with a burning in my soul to serve Jesus as my personal Savior. Scripture says, *"However, this kind does not go out except by prayer and fasting." (Matthew 17:21)*

It is important to be a clean vessel if praying for the deliverance of another. Through fasting we make room for the oppressed to go free. It is a way to deny the physical in order to focus on the spiritual. Jesus Himself fasted as a form of intercession. Before officially beginning His earthy ministry, Jesus went into the wilderness and fasted for forty days and nights. In His weakened state He was tempted by the devil, and that temptation was treacherous. Satan told Jesus, *"If thou be the Son of God, command that these stones be made bread. (Matthew 4:3)* Jesus responded by saying, *"... It is written, Man shall not live by bread alone, but by every word that proceedeth out of the mouth of*

This is Personal

God." Intercession and fasting go hand in hand. Fasting tunes our hearts to seek God's face. It awakens our senses. When we fast in intercession it is for the reverence of His truth, to break yokes and bring down barriers of resistance. "Our spiritual need is greater than our physical discomfort and the supply for both comes from God alone." When we are praying against a particular stronghold in our life or the life of another, we need to be armed for battle. Our prayers are most effective for the situation when we are exercising our faith for God's ability to deliver, our subjection to His purpose and will, and our steadfastness to entreat His help. Fasting increases our reliance on Him in the moments of physical weakness and need, it turns our mind toward God an activate our prayers to break down the bounds in which we are confound. It is in these moments we feel most intensely armed for battle. Also sometimes keeping quiet about your fast will knock Satan off your trail, loosen His grips and throw him for a loop. What you do in private God sees. No one needs to know you are fasting. "It's best sometimes not to let the rigAs the Holy Spirit leads you, make this a personal discipline between you and God. He rewards publicly what you've done in private through fasting and prayer on the behalf of another.

The Climb

Exodus 19 speaks of the time when the Israelites left Egypt and set up camp at the base of Mount Sinai. God called to Moses and asked him to climb the mountain. Moses was around eighty years old when God asked him to climb a mountain that was about six thousand feet which would have been no small task for this elderly man. He instructed Moses to come up so he could give him a message to take down to the people and once he shared the

This is Personal

message with them he wanted Moses to make the trip back up again so he could tell him how the children of Israel received the message.

Our human nature would probably be thinking, God if I heard you call out to me at the base of the mountain why couldn't you give me the message there or tell the people what you wanted them to know directly? It would have probably saved me and you some time. But Moses did not think about it in this manner he simply obeyed. I am sure Moses was tired when the Lord again instructed him to come back up and go down once more but this time to prepare (consecrate) the people for His arrival. Again, he did not allow his natural mind or his physical state to dictate his obedience. Moses went up and down Mount Sinai numerous times to bring Aaron up, to hear God, to commune with Him, receive instruction and to even write the ten commandments. As we continue to commune with God, we must be prepared for the climb.

In prayer there will be times that we have to go higher to incline our ears to hear what God is saying. Although we get weary and tired at times, when it is orchestrated by God, our spirit has no bounds. He gives strength and endurance to conquer every mountain before us. The more Moses climbed that mountain I could imagine that it gave him strength because his physical body was being toned and define by his spiritual workout. Moses was given the opportunity to present himself before the Lord every time he was called to come up. I can remember when I was in school we had to do presentations before the class and I was often nervous because all eyes were on me, but the more opportunities I got to do it I felt less nervous until one day it was no longer a factor in my mind. Why? Because I did all the necessary things before class to ensure that I would do my absolute best. Will we be great all the time? Absolutely not, but the more you climb in prayer and walk towards God voice, the atmosphere around you will begin to change. Your perspective in prayer will take on a new meaning. You cannot climb up something and not feel the elevation. Whether it be the quality of the air or the scenery change going on around you. The higher we are called up in prayer, the more change can be expected.

Our willingness to listen for His call and obedience determines the way we walk up the mountain. That is why Moses made it up and down with ease. He obeyed, consecrated himself, he confessed his sins, and washed his spiritual garments. When in prayer we must walk up the mountain sometimes to present ourselves in the holy

This is Personal

place of God. To inquire guidance or get a little bit closer to dwell and bask in His presence. Prepare yourself for where God is taking you in prayer. The expense of the journey is on Him, but the walk is on you.

Removing the Lid

Never put a lid on your prayers, leaving no room for wiggle or space to experience more or ask for more. The reason sometimes we do not get more out of our prayers is because we limit God and ask for the small when He wants to give us the big. If you limit your expectations of God, you may limit how He can work in your life and the lives of those you pray for. As an intercessor you just do not want to ask God for a bandage to patch up a wound for temporary relief, when He wills to mend the wound properly so it can be healed all the way through.

This is Personal

The word lid defines itself as a cover, usually removable or hinged. An object that can be raised and remain open until it is closed by someone or something. If we trust that God is God, then we should broaden our expectations in prayer so He can speak into our hearts. Never allow the lid of your heart to be closed but remain open for His work of abundance and not the little we expect. Think of it in this manner, as we position ourselves in prayer on our knees, our words are placed on the launching pad of Jesus Christ which holds the power to break the lid off anything that wants to conceal His revelations through prayer. God has more to teach, more to give and more for us to experience in an out of prayer. We serve a God who has immeasurable boundless power, incalculable wisdom and His understanding is infinite. Once you realize this miracles, conversion and healing can begin to happen for those you stand in the gap for because there is no limit when God is giving the access to move and expand.

The Throne of Grace

Let us then with confidence draw near to the throne of grace, that we may receive mercy and find grace to help in time of need." Hebrews 4:16

Christ reconciled us back to God an opened up the chest of grace, which makes possible the great resource of prayer. Being able to approach the throne of God in prayer is based on Christ's priestly ministry of intercession, which was through his propitiating sacrifice and present seat of the Most High Priest.

Our approach to His throne in prayer should always be in humble reverence. Giving and paying great honor and respect to our Most High God. There is no place in prayer for pride or vanity. In boldness it

This is Personal

should be, but not with impertinent. We should never be irreverent, but neither do we need to be ashamed to speak exactly what is on our hearts. When you come before God, He wants to hear exactly what you have to say. Every word that is uttered in prayer from our hearts are laid before His throne. He takes them into His possession and deals with them accordingly.

Let your prayers be brought forth with great joy because the favor that has been extended to us is of high privilege. Instead of judgement we as His children are invited to bring our requests to the King. He allows us to speak freely with Him because of the grace we received from Him. No matter if we stumble or stutter in prayer, we are not criticized but received with compassion and kindness.

This is Personal

5 For His Glory

You can ask for anything in my name, and I will do it, so that the Son can bring glory to the Father. Yes, ask me for anything in my name, and I will do it! (John 14:13-14)

The glory of God is not just a feeling, it is everything contained in the character of God. The word glory translated means *heavy weight.* God's glory has been often called the manifestation of His presence, but it is more than His presence it is His power too. Power that can bring forth resurrection, deliverance that will allow all believers to be overcomers and transformed. It is the greatest of powers that could ever exist. It is beyond any suffering or circumstances that could ever come upon us. *For I consider the suffering of this present time are not worthy to be* compared with the glory which shall be revealed in us." (Romans 8:18) It is touchable, reachable and available to all His people because you were born of God. (John 1:13)

Apostle Paul says, God's glory shall be revealed in us, so as we pray for ourselves and others may His glory be revealed to us.

Where do we see God's character most gloriously revealed? God's glory is revealed in scripture and in the man of Jesus Christ. It is in all that he has done in the coming, living, dying, rising and ascending of the Lord Jesus. He declared it with power, certainty and clarity. *"And the Word became flesh and dwelt among us, and we have seen his glory, glory as of the only Son from the Father, full of grace and truth." (John 1:14)* Through His coming and His blood shed we are redeemed and delivered from the devil's grip. When we invoke the blood of Jesus, we destroy the

This is Personal

foundation upon which the strongholds of Satan are built. Everything that God has revealed of Himself through Jesus Christ should encourage us as we pray. Apostle Paul and many other great men and women of the Bible were concerned about the glory of God. The glory of God should drive and motivate our mission in prayer. Our zeal for it should cry out as we pray to our glorious God.

How do we as intercessors pray for the glory of the Lord to come forth?

As you pray be sincere of what you request of God, He reveals to those He can trust. Ask Him to allow you to experience and see His glory as you continue to seek Him. Ask Him to allow you to know the hope of His calling, which is the hope of His glory. Pray that you will understand the riches of the glory of His inheritance in the saints, because when we inherited Him, glory was deposited in us. Lastly, pray for the insight and revelation of what it means to even walk in His glory. *God has now revealed to us his mysterious will regarding Christ- which is to fulfill his own good plan. And this is the plan: At the right time he will bring everything together under the authority of Christ- everything in heaven and on earth. Furthermore, because we are united with Christ, we have received an inheritance from God, for he chose us in advance, and he makes everything work out according to his plan. Ephesians 1:9-11*

His Glory / Our Help

One thing about God is that He displays His glory by helping rather than demanding help.

No eye has seen a God besides you, who works for those who wait for him. (Isaiah 64:4)

This verse alone if you would allow it to, it will change the way you pray as an

This is Personal

intercessor, because it requires you to look beyond yourself toward the bigger plan. The glory belongs to the Lord and not to the people who render the prayer. When we see that the plan of the Lord is not about us, but bigger than us we have a better chance to grow more spiritually. Our expectations are no longer limited to what we can do through prayer but geared towards what God can do. It is important to capture the true essence of His character in our hearts as we pray. It is God Himself who displays His glory while we get the help.

Moses asked God to "Please, show me your glory" (Exodus 33:18) and he granted his request.

When the believers gathered together in unity, seeking the Lord, the glory of the Lord appeared in the upper room on the Day of Pentecost and sat on the head of each person there. (Acts 2:1-4)

This is Personal

We as born-again believers who possess the ability to manifest God's glory here on earth, Jesus told Martha in John 11:40 that if she would believe she would see the glory of the Lord, He then raised her brother Lazarus from the dead. His glory reveals a glimpse of who He is when it is put on display. God's glory manifests the unwrapping of His identity, nature, holiness and His power. May the Father be glorified through His son Jesus Christ. Believe today in prayer that God is willing to show Himself mighty to you and others, that His mere presence will consume and captivate everything in your vicinity. The elements of God's glory cannot be limited when it is encountered. Nothing in its reach can remain the same when it is touched.

The Power of His Name

There is Power in the name of Jesus, and may His name forever be glorified in and

This is Personal

out of prayer. The power of prayer is not power that comes from the act of prayer but the flow from the one in whom we pray. When intercessors use the name of Jesus in prayer, we are asking Him to basically throw His weight around. It is not like signing off *sincerely yours*, His name is a name of authority. A name of Power, a name that cannot be classified with any other name. A name that exalts itself and forms a foundation of stability that cannot be shaken or torn down. At the mention of His name the glory of the Lord hits the earth realm and cause demons to tremble and flee. Miracle, signs and wonders occur in the church and the personal lives of other believers. His name brings forth the truth. *Not to us, Oh Lord, not to us, but to your name give glory because of your lovingkindness, because of your truth (Psalm 115).*

This is Personal

The name of Jesus revolutionizes our faith and gives us the boldness and confidence we need in prayer. His name is a strong tower and a fortress that even the darkness cannot withstand or hide from its light. Praying in Jesus name is like praying as He would, in His strength, through His spirit. Prayers released only in His name enter through the gateway of heaven because through His name lies the key to open heaven's door. *Jesus answered, I am the way and the truth and the life. No one comes to the Father except through me. (John 14:6)*

Conclusion

Change your words, Change your world, Shape your I am

I have the Favor of God.

I will live and not die.

I can do all things through Christ Jesus who strengthens me.

Prayer is never complete without a declaration of victory. We must always remember to pray from a place of victory not for victory because we serve and pray to a God that has already won.

Declarations help us call forth those things that are not as though they are. Declaring and praying over our lives and our family allows us to fill the atmosphere with God's truths and causes them to connect and attach itself to us.

As it is written, I have made you a father of many nations. In the presence of him whom believed- God, who gives life to the dead and calls those things which do not exist as though they did" (Romans 4:17).

God's method of bringing life to dead places, people, nations, gifts are often call forth by a chosen vessel who in turns goes out and speaks what God has said and brings life to what looks dead. (The essence of faith in intercession is to believe before we see, not to see to believe). When we declare things alive that look dead, we join in with God's Words in calling those things that are not as though they are.

There are several examples of biblical declarations that you can use daily as you continue to build a deeper relationship with Christ.

> **1.** I can do all things through Christ who strengthens me. ***(Philippians 4:13)***

This is Personal

2. God has not given me the spirit of fear. He gives me power, love, and self-discipline. *(2 Timothy 1:7)*

3. I shall meditate on God's word day and night. I am successful and prosperous. *(Psalm 1:2-3, Joshua 1:8)*

4. I give and receive. Good measure, pressed down, shaken together, running over, it will be put into my lap. *(Luke 6:38)*

5. I am blessed when I come in and blessed when I go out. *(Deuteronomy 28:6)*

6. The Lord has established me as a holy person to Himself. I keep His commandments and walk in His ways. *(Deuteronomy 28:9)*

7. But by God's doing I am in Christ Jesus. He became to me wisdom, righteousness, sanctification, and redemption. *(1 Corinthians 1:30)*

8. The joy of the Lord is my strength. *(Nehemiah 8:10)*

This is Personal

9. I speak God's word and hearing the word increases my faith. *(Romans 10:17)*

10. Christ bore my sins in His own body on the cross and I am healed by His stripes. *(1 Peter 2:24)*

This is Personal

Listed below are a few important scriptures that every intercessor needs to know which will help them in their walk as they keep God's word planted in their hearts.

- **Establish and Maintain a Personal Relationship with Jesus Christ** – *But if you remain in me and my words remain in you, you may ask for anything you want, and it will be granted! (John 15:7)*

- **The Will of God-** *And we are confident that he hears us whenever we ask for anything that pleases him. And since we know he hears us when we make our requests, we also know that he will give us what we ask for. (1 John 5:14-15)*

- **Ask – Seek – Knock** – *Keep on asking, and you will receive what you ask for. Keep on seeking, and you will find. Keep on knocking, and the door will be opened to you. 8 For everyone who asks, receives. Everyone who seeks, finds. And to everyone who knocks, the door will be opened. (Matthew 7:7-8)*

- **God will Hear the Prayers of the Righteous-** *The LORD is far from the wicked, but he hears the prayers of the righteous. (Proverbs 15:29)* Confess your sins to each other and pray for each other so that you may be healed. The earnest prayer of a righteous person has great power and produces wonderful results. *(James 5:16)*

- **Prayer of Agreement-** *I also tell you this: If two of you agree here on earth concerning anything you ask, my Father in heaven will do it for you. (Matthew 18:19)*

- **Do not Lose Heart-** *One day Jesus told his disciples a story to show that they should always pray and never give up. ² "There was a judge in a certain city," he said, "who neither feared God nor cared about people. ³ A widow of that city came to him repeatedly, saying, 'Give me justice in this dispute with my enemy.' ⁴ The judge ignored her for a while, but finally he said to himself, 'I don't fear God or care about people, ⁵ but this woman is driving me crazy. I'm going to see that she gets justice, because she is*

This is Personal

*wearing me out with her constant requests!"
(Luke 18:1-8)*

6 Then the Lord said, "Learn a lesson from this unjust judge. 7 Even he rendered a just decision in the end. So, don't you think God will surely give justice to his chosen people who cry out to him day and night? Will he keep putting them off? 8 I tell you; he will grant justice to them quickly! But when the Son of Man[a] returns, how many will he find on the earth who have faith?"

- **Pray to God the Father in the Name of Jesus-** *You can ask for anything in my name, and I will do it, so that the Son can bring glory to the Father. 14 Yes, ask me for anything in my name, and I will do it! (John 14:13-14)* 23 At that time you won't need to ask me for anything. I tell you the truth, you will ask the Father directly, and he will grant your request because you use my name. 24 You haven't done this before. Ask, using my name, and you will receive, and you will have abundant joy. *(John 16: 23-24)*

This is Personal

Know Your Authority

Many of us are being held captive spiritually, not because of the enemy's power, but because we do not clearly understand our authority and calling in Christ.

God has called you out from among the world and separated you to make a difference. Whether it be in your family, your community, this country or even this nation. He has called you to go out and make a change through prayer in the earth realm. God could go out and enforce His will, but He limits His dealings on earth by working through His people. He did not create us to be passive but to be a bold people who will stand and bring forth His will.

He has given us the authority to break the personal strongholds in our lives and the lives of others. Although the world lies in the power of the evil one (1 John 5:19)

...Because greater is he that is in you, than he that is in the world. (1 John 4:4) Jesus has the authority in heaven and earth, He rules through the church; and guess what that church is you and I and all others who believe He is our Lord and Savior. He changes things on earth through us! We must learn to exercise our authority right in the middle of Satan's territory and dismantle His plans through the power of prayer.

We do this by:

- **Abiding in Christ-** *Allowing all things to flow from Him; it will enable you to pray the things that are on God's heart.*

- **Be Steadfast in Prayer and Ready at All Times for the Battle-** *Know that you are in the enemy territory. Know that whether you want to engage in war or not he is not going to let up. Be strong and courageous, you are here to fight for God's Kingdom in prayer.*

This is Personal

Hold up your Shield of Faith which blocks you from the fiery darts of the enemy.

- **Standing on God's Promises**- *The work has been done; the foundation you stand on was form through the hands of God and finished by the work of Jesus Christ. He has given a sturdy and solid ground that does not shake, change, or become dismantled.*

- **Know and Pray God's Word**- *The truth is what the enemy does not want you to know. The less you know the weaker you are. **Read it, Speak it, Meditate on it day and night.** Allow it to become part of your every being. Declarative prayer is key when exercising your authority (Ex. Daniel 9:3-19).*

- **Fasting on a Regular Basis**- *Fasting and prayer together brings on spiritual power and strength. Fasting clears the mind while praying feeds and strengthen the soul.*

- **Letting God's Peace Reign in Your Heart**- *Take on an attitude of peace and joy (Colossians 3:15).*

This is Personal

What should I pray for?

Here's a short guide that you can use to assist you in Intercession

As you enter intercession, pray for:

- The church in all places, and especially your own church home and the congregation.

- The nations of the world, your own nation, and all those in authority; President, Congress and Senate etc.

- All leaders who labor in their calling; Apostles, Prophets, Evangelist, Pastors, Teachers etc.

- Concerns of the local community.

- Those who are suffering or in trouble.

- Any prayer burden that has been bought on by the Holy Spirit.

- Requests that have been given to you from another.

  - Pray also for the protection of other intercessors who are laboring on the

This is Personal

battlefield in prayer. Pray that more intercessors will arise and stand in the gap for others and for God's will to come forth.

There's More Than One Way

There are many different types of Prayer as the Bible reveals in *1 Timothy 2:1 "I urge, then, first of all, that petitions, prayers, intercession and thanksgiving be made for all people.* Here I have taken the time and listed below the main types of prayer along with a scriptural home of an example in the Bible that you can be refreshed by or gain further knowledge for the growth of your ministry in the area of prayer.

- **Prayer of Faith** – All prayer should be given in faith. It is given in utter dependence and submission, believing our God is sovereign and good. (James 5:15)

This is Personal

- **Prayer of Worship**- Words of adoration that acknowledge and glorify who God is. It is a praise of His attributes and His love. It magnifies and exalts His majesty and esteems His name. (Acts 13:2-3)

- **Prayer of Thanksgiving**- It is receiving God's gift and giving thanks for His loving kindness. Through thanks we recognize and acknowledge that every good and perfect thing comes from God. (Philippians 4:6)

- **Prayer of Confession/Consecration**- This is offered when we are convicted of sins as we are remorseful of having sinned against God. He does not desire us to live with a downcast heart, He is a merciful and forgiving God. If we allow Him to wash away our sins. (Psalm 32:5) Consecration- Prayer of re-dedication or renewed devotion to love and serve Him more. (Matthew 26:36-45)

- **Prayer of Petition or Supplication**- Let your request be known to God. Ask

This is Personal

and it should be giving in accordance to His will. (1 John 5:14-15)

- **Prayer of Intercession**- Prayers offered on the behalf of others. Intercessory prayer is a ministry of Christian fellowship that reminds us of our union with other believers. (1 Timothy 2:1; John 17)

- **Prayer of Agreement** (also known as Corporate Prayer)- In Him we are one with each other and we are instructed to pray together. A bond of two is stronger than of one. (Acts 1:14; Matthew 18:19)

- Lastly the Bible also speaks about Praying in the Spirit- when you do not know what to pray or lack the words for the circumstance or situation. Prayer is a conversation with God and in our weakness and lack the Holy Spirit Himself makes intercessions for us. (Romans 8:26-27)

This is Personal

You were born and purposed for Prayer and Built for the fight. Greater is He that is in you than He that is in the world.

This is Personal

Final Thoughts

A Word from the Author ~

When we allow God into our lives and build relationship with Him, we mature and grow in greater understanding of what He is like and what He thinks about us. This helps us to know His heart and pray for His will to come forth. One of the greatest abilities that I have learned when it comes to prayer, is to be still and listen.

Allowing your heart to be still before God and inclining your ears to hear His voice gives us a chance to hear what He wants to do in any situation. It brings us to a place where we no longer see ourselves, situations or circumstances. All that matters is that we are engaging the Spirit of God.

I pray that this book is beneficial to you. I pray that it will allow you to rekindle a bond with our Heavenly Father and dig deeper into your prayer life. It is my prayer

This is Personal

that you will take on a new boldness and confidence before His throne as you intercede on the behalf of your love ones, community and nation. God wants and awaits to hear from you, so let your heart intertwine with His through prayer so that His will, will flow to the hearts of His people.

Always remember that Intercessory Prayer is not just requesting and petitioning but it is a lifestyle of consecration and yielding.

- Prayer is always about Jesus from Beginning to End. He stirs it, authors it and answers it.

- Prayer holds no weigh without faith. They must work together to bring forth what God desires for our lives.

- A praying life lands you right in the midst of God's will for earth. So be bold and full of confidence when you

This is Personal

approach the Throne of Grace He is waiting and wants to hear from you.

- Prayer is a privilege that we all have no one is denied from rendering it. It is accessible 24/7.

- When you turn your thoughts and words toward God's direction, it has become prayer. You are now in a place of counsel. You have made the decision to involve God to change your heart to match His will.

- Prayer is a powerful weapon that allows us to engage in war without even going out physically to the battlefield, it is a gateway in which we bring the battlefield to God to allow Him to take care of the war for us.

This is Personal

"Always pray with a purpose."

The secret to meaningful prayer is not what you say or how you say it, but that you go in it with a purpose, which is to talk to your Father in Heaven. He has given you scriptures to learn, the gospel to help you grow, the ability through his Son, Jesus Christ which grants us access. Access to purposely move and inquire of His counsel. To think on purpose, to clear your mind for purpose, to pour your heart out on purpose to make room for His purpose. To know God on purpose through prayer.

About the Author

Tieka M. Bonaparte

Evangelist Tieka Bonaparte was born in Orangeburg, South Carolina and grew up in the small town of Fort Motte, South Carolina. Tieka was ordained as a Pastor in 2018. She is the Co-Founder and Co-Pastor of Faith Word Outreach Ministries in Harrisburg, North Carolina. She is the Co-Author of *Living by Faith: Awaking the Eyes of Faith 21 Day Devotional*. In addition, Tieka is also the President of Created for Purpose and Co-Founder of the Movement: I Come Alive in which she travels to awaken and revive the hearts of those who have fallen asleep in the Kingdom. She is the loving wife of Senior Pastor Travis Bonaparte. Tieka is a loving and caring mother of four wonderful children. She is truly a worshipper and servant at heart. Tieka is filled with the

This is Personal

Holy Spirit and passionate about bringing hearts before the throne room of God through the ministry of Intercession. She has learned firsthand what it means to have a heart for God's use. She is currently training prayer intercessors to stand on the wall for the Kingdom of God as they become effective in prayer. Tieka is an anointed woman of God and loves Him with all her heart.

For Speaking Engagements, Please Contact:

Evangelist Tieka Bonaparte

Faith Word Outreach Ministries

P.O Box 692

Harrisburg N.C 28075

Email- info@faithwordoutreach.org

Also Check out the website:

www.faithwordoutreach.org

This is Personal